Northern Flight of Dreams

**FLYING ADVENTURES IN
BRITISH COLUMBIA, YUKON,
NW TERRITORIES AND ALASKA**

OTHER WORKS BY THE AUTHOR

Flight of the Red Beaver: A Yukon Adventure

This is the story of the author's adventures as a bush pilot flying his favorite ship, the red de Havilland Beaver float plane CF-IBP, and ski planes into the vast northern wilderness of British Columbia, the Yukon, and the Northwest Territories. It's also the story of the fulfillment of a boyhood dream: to go north, build a log cabin, and live off the land.

Northern Flight of Dreams (Video)

This video covers the last 10 chapters of this book and was filmed in July and August of 1993. It brings to life the Yukon, Northwest Territories, British Columbia and Alaska, as mentioned in both books, and shows the red de Havilland Beaver CF-IBP landing, loading up, and departing the Watson Lake Flying Service Float Plane Base.

Lars Larson, Yukon Bush Pilot (fiction work in progress)

This novel is the story of Lars Larson, a young American man just out of high school, who heads north to the Yukon to become a bush pilot and to search for his father who he has never met. When World War II breaks out, Lars joins the Royal Canadian Air Force and flies Spitfires in the Battle of Britain. He later joins the United States Navy and flies fighters off an aircraft carrier in the Pacific against the Japanese. After the war, while flying a Beaver float plane to supply a firefighting crew on a river, he meets Michelle, a woman with long dark hair and dark brown eyes.

Northern Flight of Dreams

FLYING ADVENTURES IN BRITISH COLUMBIA, YUKON, NW TERRITORIES AND ALASKA

By Larry Whitesitt

MB MARQUETTE BOOKS SPOKANE, WA

Printed in the United States of America

Library of Congress Cataloging-in-Publication Data

Whitesitt, Larry, 1938-
   Northern flight of dreams : flying adventures in British Columbia, Yukon,
NW territories, and Alaska / by Larry Whitesitt.
      p. cm.
   Includes index.
   ISBN 0-922993-09-2 (pbk. : alk. paper)
   1. British Columbia--Description and travel. 2. Canada, Northern--
Description and travel. 3. Alaska--Description and travel. 4. Whitesitt, Larry,
1938---Travel--British Columbia. 5. Whitesitt, Larry, 1938---Travel--Canada,
Northern. 6. Whitesitt, Larry, 1938---Travel--Alaska. 7. Bush flying--British
Columbia. 8. Bush flying--Canada, Northern. 9. Bush flying--Alaska. 10. Bush
pilots--United States--Biography. I. Title.
   F1087.W48 2004
   917.1904'4--dc22

                                                        2003027352

MARQUETTE BOOKS
3107 E. 62nd Avenue
Spokane, WA 99223
509-443-7057
books@marquettebooks.org
www.MarquetteBooks.org

To my grandchildren, Daniel, Kaitlyn and Gavin,
who are my hiking, fishing and kayaking partners;
to my son, Scott, a fellow pilot and
cheerful companion on northern trails;
and to his lovely wife, Stacy.

Illustration of two loons
("Voice of the Wilderness")
By Scott Whitesitt

C ONTENTS

Preface, 9

Map of Flight Route, 11

Chapter 1
Spirits of the North, 13

Chapter 2
Adventures on the Open Road, 31

Chapter 3
Olympic Rain Forest, 53

Chapter 4
Harrison, Lake Coeur d'Alene, and the Open Road, 61

Chapter 5
Grand Canyon and Bisbee, 81

Chapter 6
Flying North into the Past, 93

Chapter 7
Flying Over the Rockies, 107

Chapter 8
Magic of the Yukon, 123

Chapter 9
Flight to Dawson City, 133

Chapter 10
Spirits of Deadmen Valley, 145

Chapter 11
Fort Liard, Northwest Territories, 155

Chapter 12
Flying Across British Columbia, 161

Chapter 13
Atlin, Gem of the North, 173

Chapter 14
Skagway, Gate to the Yukon, 181

Chapter 15
Return to Atlin, 187

Chapter 16
Wilderness Flight Home, 193

Epilogue, 205

Name Index, 213

Subject Index, 217

About the Author, 224

PREFACE

This story begins September 8, 1989, in the cockpit of Cessna 734 Uniform Whiskey. It was a bright, sunny afternoon as we flew over Arctic rivers and lakes in Canada's North, remembering earlier times when I flew float planes into this vast wilderness. The word "we" is often used, which refers to the unity of the plane and me.

The flight took me as far north as the Arctic coastline to the Inuit village of Tuktoyaktuk, Northwest Territories, and then west to the log cabin Indian village of Old Crow, which is the farthest northern settlement in the Yukon.

A short time after returning to my hometown of Spokane, Washington, from that northern flight, I completed and self-published *Flight of the Red Beaver,* my first book. The day after the second printing of the book came off the press, I departed Spokane on a 50,000-mile journey down the highway in my blue Buick full of books. This adventure across the Western United States and into Canada, autographing books and sharing my memories of the north, took almost a year.

I wanted to make one more flight to the Yukon and record the north on film. On July 28, 1993, I was most fortunate to depart runway 26 at Spokane's Felts Field and fly to the Yukon in a small plane with photographer Janey Youngblood. As I wrote in my notebook journal, my friend began recording on film this northern flight of dreams. This book is the written record of that journey.

Special thanks to Janey Youngblood for all the typing and revisions she did on this manuscript, and for the photographs that were taken on the last 10 chapters of this book as she filmed the video, *Northern Flight of Dreams.*

9

Thanks also to Barbara Chamberlain for the first editing of the manuscript and to Nadine Cobb for the final editing.

Finally, I would like to thank my son, Scott, for the drawing of the loons which is shown on page 5.

Larry Whitesitt
December 2003
Spokane, Washington

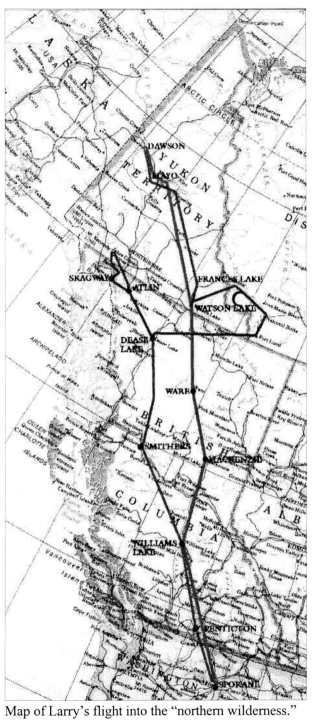

Map of Larry's flight into the "northern wilderness."

CHAPTER 1

Spirits of the North

Arctic rivers flow wild and free as they wind through timbered valleys on their journey to the distant Beaufort Sea. Lakes reflect the deep blue sky. The warm, friendly September sun brings back fond memories as Canada's north slips beneath the white wings of the plane.

Near the headwaters of the Eagle River along the eastern edge of the Continental Divide, several lakes appear as a beautiful, rugged land unfolds. This area of the Cassiar Mountains in British Columbia lies in a vast wilderness known as the Northern Rocky Mountains, home to the grizzly bear, wolf, moose, deer, stone sheep, mountain goat, caribou, bald eagle, and the loon, the voice of the wilderness.

The Northern Rocky Mountain wilderness area begins north of British Columbia's Peace River country and extends to the Liard River, just south of the Yukon border and west of the Alaska Highway to the Cassiar Mountains.

Arctic rivers in this area are all free-flowing, without dams, including the Kechika, which is 40 miles east and drains the Rocky Mountain Trench northwest from Sifton Pass into the Liard (sometimes referred to as the west branch of the Mackenzie) and the Mackenzie River itself. What geologists call the Rocky Mountain Trench is 900 miles long, running in a northwest direction in the eastern part of British Columbia from the Montana border almost to the Liard River just south of the Yukon border.

Today a dam spans the Peace River on the east side of the Rocky Mountains, just west of Hudson Hope. The huge reservoir is called Williston Lake and it covers the lower portion of the Finlay River.

In the late 1990s, a large Class A provincial parkland of 1.17 million hectares (2.89 million acres) was set aside in the Northern Rocky Mountains — British Columbia's largest single designation of preserved wilderness. Because of the wide variety of large animals found there, this region is sometimes called "the Serengeti of North America."

In the 1960s and 1970s, I was most fortunate to be a bush pilot in Canada and had the wonderful experience of flying float planes and ski planes into rivers and lakes in the northern Rocky Mountain wilderness, often with my cheerful son, Scott, as copilot.

Now, adventure was thick in the air as we, my faithful ship 734 Uniform Whiskey and I, flew from Watson Lake, Yukon Territory, toward the Dease Lake Airport in British Columbia, Canada. It was a sunny Friday afternoon on September 8, 1989, as we continued flying across the north.

This northern flight had begun one week earlier at Felts Field in my hometown of Spokane, Washington, where I rented a Cessna 172, 734 Uniform Whiskey. From Spokane we flew as far north as Fort St. John, British Columbia, where I spent the night. The following morning, after waiting several hours for the weather to lift, we flew to a settlement called Fort Simpson, Northwest Territories, which is located on the banks of the Mackenzie River. Fort Simpson is situated on an island at the junction of the Liard and Mackenzie rivers. The first fort here, Fort of the Forks, was established by the Northwest Company in 1804. In 1821 the Hudson Bay Company built a post here and named it for George Simpson, the Hudson Bay Company governor.

After refueling, we followed the mighty Mackenzie River north to the oil refining town of Norman Wells, where I landed and refueled again. About fifty miles upstream is the Indian village called Fort Norman. In the early 1970s I flew into Fort Norman during the summer months and noticed many sled dogs tied up behind the Indian homes. At that time, sled dogs were used almost exclusively for winter travel. Today, sled dogs are bred to race, but snowmobiles are used in the winter for transportation. Federal law requires the Inuits to use dog teams when hunting the polar bear, to give the bear a chance. After leaving Norman Wells, we flew near the Indian village of Fort Good Hope and a short time later crossed the Arctic Circle. As we neared the Arctic coast, many lakes passed beneath our wings. About 10 p.m. I saw for the first time the Arctic Ocean, glistening in the evening sun like fine-cut diamonds.

This photo, which was taken by Larry on September 2, 1989, shows the Inuit village of Tuktoyaktuk, located on the shores of the Beaufort Sea (Arctic Ocean).

After landing at the Inuit village of Tuktoyaktuk, I obtained a room, which was quite expensive. We were weathered in at Tuk for two days and then flew to Inuvic under a low overcast sky that at times dropped its grey curtain to the treeless tundra below.

From Inuvic we flew west across the incredible 10,000 square mile Mackenzie River delta, a maze of channels and wetlands, and then over the Richardson Mountains to the farthest northern settlement in the Yukon, the log cabin Indian village of Old Crow. The Indians there were bringing in freshly caught salmon and moose for their winter meat. They were waiting for the migration of the Porcupine caribou herd, some 180,000 strong, as they still depended on the caribou for much of their meat.

The next day we flew south to Dawson City, heart of the Klondike, where the last and greatest gold rush of all time took place. I spent a few days at Dawson City taking pictures and reliving memories of other flights to this historical place. Once I flew a de Havilland Beaver float plane to Dawson and landed on the Yukon River in front of the town. From Dawson City we flew south to Whitehorse, the capitol of the Yukon. After refueling and eating lunch at the airport, we flew some 240 miles southeast to Watson Lake, where I spent the night.

After leaving Watson Lake we flew a southerly heading and crossed the Liard River in Northern British Columbia. The headwaters of the Liard, sometimes referred to as the west branch of the Mackenzie, begin about 130 miles northwest of Watson Lake in the Yukon Territory. About a half hour later we began following the Dease River, just west of the Horse Ranch Range. I thought about the wonderful gift I had received the previous night as I walked down the Alaska Highway on Watson Lake's main street to the log hotel. The night sky had lighted up in a wonderful display of the northern lights, a special gift which brought back thoughts of other magical nights I'd seen as a bush pilot.

This was familiar country and it brought back a wellspring of good memories — yet it felt like a dream, not quite the same as before. McDame, Meek Lake, Eagle River passed, and soon the clear waters of beautiful Dease Lake appeared. We flew around the southern end where George Dalziel's summer home used to be. The lake was fairly calm and I flew about a mile west to land at the Dease Lake Airport after a flight of 1.1 hours. Dease Lake drains into the Arctic watershed. A few miles south and west is the Pacific watershed. The nearby Stikine River drains into the Pacific Ocean near Wrangell, Alaska.

It was quiet at the airport — only natural sounds could be heard. I called a fuel number, and a woman arrived; however, she did not have the correct fuel key so we had to return to her office. I caught a ride with her to Dease Lake.

"The waters of this lake are so clear that people still use it for drinking water," she said. There were some new log cabins along the southern end — at least they were new since I had last been here in 1975. Dalziel's old summer log home was still standing on the sandy south shoreline, but it was badly deteriorated and boarded up.

The late George Dalziel, "Dal," was a well-known big game guide and an old-time bush pilot who did some of the first flying over the Mackenzie Mountains in the 1930s. Dal lived about a thousand lives; he was a fascinating man and legend of the north. In the 1930s, he shot game and flew it into mining camps for their food. Dal started B.C. Yukon Air Service at Watson Lake about 1948. He purchased the newly built de Havilland Beavers straight from the factory.

When I first went to the Yukon in 1969, I flew Beavers for B.C. Yukon. At the time, it was owned by two cousins by the name of Harrison. Ernie Harrison, an easygoing, well-liked pilot, ran the operation and did some of the flying.

In 1970 I flew B.C. Yukon's single-engine Otter into Blue Sheep Lake where Dal had a cabin. My son, Scott, and wife, Kathy, flew with me that flight. We had to fly low, through a narrow, winding canyon so that we wouldn't overshoot the pond-sized lake. The lake appeared suddenly around a bend, and we made a short lake landing. I flew into several lakes to deliver Dal's hunters during the busy hunting seasons in the early 1970s. In the summer of 1970, Kathy worked for George Dalziel at Watson Lake, transporting hunters and camp supplies to the float plane base.

After I spent some time looking at Dease Lake and remembering the past, the fuel woman drove me back to the plane. I topped the tanks and we were soon airborne for Telegraph Creek, fifty-five miles southwest. We flew over the Tanzilla River most of the way, which is paralleled by the road from Dease Lake to Telegraph Creek on the west side. The Grand Canyon of the Stikine begins just east of my course, thirty miles below Dease Lake. It is a fantastic, deep, wild-looking canyon I've flown over and appreciated often. I marvelled again at the churning wild waters of the Stikine as it shot through this narrow canyon on its turbulent journey to the sea.

After a thirty-minute flight over some rugged but familiar country, the new airstrip appeared. It bordered the road on the south side and lay between the road and the river a few miles east of Telegraph Creek. There was no noticeable wind as I circled the gravel strip. I elected to land toward the west, made a short field landing, and touched down just past the end of the strip a few feet beyond the bushes bordering the end of the runway.

Again, as at Dease Lake, the blanket of silence surrounded me. Walking toward town after securing my plane, I felt as if I was in a world where time slowed down, the way I'd felt when I was a boy. The gravel road led me by a helicopter office and then by a log cabin that said "Tahltan Outfitters." Several smaller log cabins were strung out to the west. I talked to a young man outside the cabin who said this was Fletcher Day's home.

"Oh, I know him; I used to fly for Watson Lake Flying Service and flew Fletcher out in the bush for several years," I said.

The young man said, "Fletcher is coming in by seaplane this evening from his hunting camp. One of his guides, Charley Smith, drowned at

Victoria Lake, and his funeral is tomorrow at the Tahltan Indian Village."

"Tell Fletcher I'll try to see him while I'm here. Could you tell me the best way to get to town?" I asked.

"Oh, you can take a shortcut on the Indian trail that starts off the road over there. It's a good trail," he assured me.

The trail began under a bluff. On my left towards the river it had sloughed and was almost vertical. One slip and I figured if I wasn't killed, I'd be so banged up that I would wish I had been. A trek that seemed to last forever finally ended at the edge of town, down the steep mountainside close to the river. I wondered to myself if this Indian was trying to get rid of this white man, or just testing his surefootedness. Guess I'll never know.

At about 1830 in the evening I arrived at the Riversong Café. This had been the original Hudson Bay Store when I flew into Telegraph Creek in the late 1960s and 1970s. I had dealt mostly with the owner of the other store a block upriver, who would drive up to Sawmill Lake on top of the hill when I landed the Beaver and give me a lift to town, bringing me fuel if I needed it. I think he did most of the business at that time in Telegraph Creek.

I obtained a room at the Riversong Café and Hotel in one of the adjoining old Hudson Bay buildings. The shower and toilet were in the main building that was also the store and café. The room was clean and had cold running water, a stove, refrigerator, couch and bed, all for a very reasonable thirty-five dollars. At least it was reasonable compared to some other places in the north that I had experienced on this trip!

The sun was getting low and I wanted to get as many pictures as I could before it set. I did not know how long I would be here or what the weather tomorrow would bring. With my camera in hand I began the steep journey up the road to the Tahltan Indian village. It was near the top of the hill overlooking the town site from on high. I knew the graveyard was just behind the village on a knoll with a wonderful view of the Stikine River and Telegraph Creek below.

A teenaged boy and friend gave me a short lift in an old car. I asked him, "Do you know a retired Tahltan Indian that spends his winters in Seattle?"

"Sure, that's my uncle," he said.

My son, Scott, said he had worked out one winter in Seattle with this retired gentleman, lifting weights. Scott said, "He was in excellent condition — tall, strong, full head of hair and looked much younger than his years. He returns to Telegraph Creek every summer and hunts there in the fall."

This is the former Hudson Bay store, and in the background is the old storage building where Larry stayed and saw the "spirit owl."

The car barely ran and belched blue smoke up through the floorboard. I walked most of the way; the exercise was good for me since I had been sitting in my flying machine on most of this trip.

As I walked through the Indian village I was joined by a village dog that became my companion to the graveyard. When Scott and I had flown in here in 1975 there had been spirit houses over most of the graves. I was disappointed to find only one left and was glad to record it on film before it disappeared into the earth. It was constructed of wood and had an iron fence around it. Some of the graves were from the middle of the last century.

After walking around the old part of the cemetery, I sat down with my new companion and took in the view. Downstream toward the west, the mighty Stikine River contrasted with the doll-sized houses of Telegraph Creek. I offered two green grapes to my brown furry friend, who spit them on the ground after his first taste. When nothing more was forthcoming, he gingerly picked them up again. Once he decided that they weren't so bad, it took him only fifteen minutes to finish off my sack of grapes.

The sun was setting over the western peaks. I quietly felt the presence of the sacred last resting place of these Tahltan Indians. It was a quiet place, perched on a point of land with an eagle's view of the winding Stikine River below. Its steep hillsides joined the tree-covered banks before disappearing into the swift waters beyond. The scene was framed by rising mountains far to the west and beyond the last bend in the river.

In the Indian village, my hiking companion was called home by a native man, and we parted company.

I wrote in my journal:

Friday, September 8, 2230: *Think I will leave early and try to get home tomorrow. I am so tired. Time to go home, I've accomplished what I set out to do and a little more. It's been a good trip, weather is great here. Don't think I would want to be a pilot full time again no way even a week of flying is really getting tiring.*

Saturday, September 9: *My sleep was restless. My eyes opened and I looked out the window above my bed. A brilliant white owl was suspended in the air, looking at me. Perhaps giving me a message, a warning go back to sleep, delay my departure. The owl floated sideways and disappeared. I was rubbing my eyes. Was it a dream? But I was awake!*

I slept in and felt fit, relaxed. Did the right thing!

Sitting on a bench in front of the old Hudson Bay store, the warm sun feels good. The muddy waters of the Stikine, slipping by quietly, quickly as the current is quite strong. I hear the distant chatter of a squirrel and a child's voice distinctly. A few noises of man, a car starting up, black flies and a few mosquitoes. Fall is later here than Dawson City.

Store doesn't open until 11 and I need film. Trying to decide if I should fly to Atlin or straight to Smithers and home.

I wondered about the Spirit Owl that had looked so intently into my eyes. It wasn't a threatening stare, but a warning look of concern. I stood up and interrupted my river watching and reflections. An old building upriver that said "River Excursions" sat next to a boat, the Trina Anne. I introduced myself to the proprietor of the place, Frances Gleason, a Tahltan Indian.

"Could you tell me the name of the man who used to run the private store here? I used to fly in here in the 1960s and 1970s," I asked.

"Sure, this building of mine is Doug Blanchard's old store. I bought it from Doug. He lives down river now, kind of retired but works some. This is the oldest building in Telegraph Creek. It used to belong to Steel Hyland and before that it belonged to Steel's father. Doug bought it from Steel Hyland, then later bought the Hudson Bay Store. I was born by that church," and he pointed to a stately Anglican Church that looked like the ones in

In the foreground is the Anglican Church, and two buildings behind that is Steel Hyland's old store, the oldest building in Telegraph Creek. On the hill behind the cross is the Indian Cemetery.

Tuktoyaktuk and Old Crow.

"Well, thanks for the information. I'm going to see Fletcher Day. I used to fly for him when I flew out of Watson Lake."

After getting some film at the Old Hudson Bay Store, I began my walk. Frances picked me up a few minutes later and gave me a lift to Fletcher Day's log home, which was surrounded by cars. The crowd was preparing for the funeral of Fletcher's guide, Charley Smith.

I saw a familiar face and asked, "Are you Fletcher Day?"

"No, he's my dad. I'll get him." Fletcher's son was the image of his father, a handsome, tall, well-built man. I saw Fletcher come out the door and his warm, friendly grin spread from ear to ear.

"Hi, Larry, how are you?" as we shook hands.

"It's been a long time, Fletcher. It's good to see you."

Fletcher told me the story of Charley's death. "We were camped at Victoria Lake, and I asked Charley to go check on the horses, like he had been doing for several days. Charley took the boat and motor, even though I cautioned him against it. The water was rough and the wind strong. All the weight was in the back of the boat, and the front end was high. I think a gust of wind must have caught the front end and flipped it over. We were fortunate to have found his body on a ledge in shallow water. Just past that ledge there is a drop-off into deep water."

Fletcher had to excuse himself to attend the funeral. This tall, intelligent, warm-hearted Tahltan had always been a pleasure to fly for.

As I prepared for my departure, sweat dripped down my forehead and ran down my back, dampening my shirt beneath the high noon sun. My ship, Cessna 734 Uniform Whiskey, waited silently at the west end of this new Telegraph Creek airstrip, a mile east of the Indian village. I used to fly into a much shorter strip years ago, north of the town by Sawmill Lake. Flying a seaplane into Sawmill Lake put a lump into my throat the first few times I took off because it's so short; however, because it's only 500 feet above sea level, the heavier dense air increased the lift and made it a safe lake to operate from.

No human sounds could be heard and the wonderful blanket of silence penetrated my being as I approached the airplane, surrounded by a northern wilderness. My spirits soared and juices flowed as I mentally prepared for the next leg of this incredible journey and the fulfillment of a dream that began many years ago.

After untying the ropes from the metal rings at the top of the wing struts, I began my walk around for the preflight inspection of my craft, looking carefully for any damage or anything that did not look right. I visually checked the wing tanks to make sure we had sufficient fuel, drained some gas into a glass bottle to check for dirt or water because contamination could cause a problem, then checked the tires and the oil.

Everything looked shipshape. I climbed aboard through the left door, strapped myself into the left-hand pilot's seat, and prepared for another flight. Mixture rich, carb heat off, master switch on, four shots of prime, throttle cracked open. "Prop clear!" I yelled out the window to advise people in the vicinity that the engine was about to start and that they should stay clear of the prop.

When I turned the ignition to the far right, the starter kicked over and the engine sputtered to life, coughed and then settled down to a familiar roar. The oil pressure looked good as we taxied to the west end of the airstrip. I began my personal check list in conjunction with the printed checklist in the plane: controls, instruments, gas, flaps, trim, prop, run-up CIGFTPR.

Pointing the nose of my craft eastward down the center of the runway,

This is Edizza Peak, 9,140 feet high, where a massive glacier covers the top of an old volcano.

I slowly eased the throttle wide open and held the elevator control column back to keep the nose high and hopefully prevent the prop from picking up loose gravel and getting nicked. We began rolling slowly at first, but the controls came to life quickly and at an air speed of fifty-five knots we became airborne and entered another world: a world of deep blue skies above a vast northern wilderness.

The time is 1247, September 9, 1989, as my ship and I leave the spirits of Telegraph Creek behind. After a few minutes we began a climbing right turn to our new heading 121°. Our course will take us on our next leg, 275 miles south over some remote glacier-covered mountains direct to Smithers, British Columbia, where we will refuel.

My ship and I were once again free of earthly bonds as we climbed toward a speck that in time became a massive glacier covering the top of an old volcano named Edizza Peak, 9,140 feet high. Several good-sized lakes in the valley to the east border the foot of this massive peak. Kinaskan Lake, where I sometimes overnighted at Steel Hyland's lodge, is eighteen miles southeast of my position. Steel was a well-known old-timer that I had known for many years. I remember his happy, friendly greeting when I would drop

Bowser Lake is about 20 miles long. The haze in the background was caused by slash burns. This was the first sign of pollution after leaving the Artic Ocean.

in, landing on the lake and spending the night. His wonderful wife, Lou, was an excellent cook and a pleasant, open and warm hostess. They have both passed away now, but their memory lives on in the people of the North who knew this remarkable, friendly couple.

Steel's father, and after him Steel, owned and operated a store that was the oldest building in Telegraph Creek, as well as a trading post at Hyland Post just east of Coldfish Lake in a wilderness setting some sixty or seventy miles east of my position. That was many years ago and it has long been deserted.

Unnamed glaciers beneath towering mountains can be seen in every direction. Sixty-five miles west is an ice field that is over one hundred miles long and runs in a northwesterly direction It is made up of Sawyer Glaciers, Baird Glaciers and several other glaciers, with mountain peaks towering 10,000 feet and higher. A line on my WAC chart divides the glaciers, part of which lie in Alaska, but with the largest portion in British Columbia, Canada.

Our altitude was 10,000 feet as we flew a few miles east of Bowser Lake, which is about twenty miles long if you follow the bow in the lake, or

This is a simple cabin Larry built in the Kispiox Valley in the summer of 1964. He and his family lived off the land and ate moose and fish.

twelve miles if you fly straight from east to west. About twenty miles south we crossed the Nass River, a few miles west of Meziadin Lake.

The sky became hazy with smoke due to the massive slash burns, common this time of year in the logged areas. At first I thought it was pollution from pulp mills and cities farther south. It was so disappointing to leave the clear blue skies behind and have to deal with humankind's dirty skies once again. I hate pollution and human disregard for the environment, so prevalent in the United States.

Stevens Lake appeared, rounded and spread out like a photo taken from a satellite. Pulling the throttle back a bit, I began the descent. I wanted to fly low over the Kispiox Valley and hopefully spot the simple cabin built with my own hands in the summer of 1964, shortly after arriving as landed immigrants in Canada with my four-year-old son, Scott and my wife, Kathy. She was an excellent mother with a good pioneering spirit and I don't recall her complaining about the primitive conditions.

We hauled water in buckets from the Kispiox River for all our needs. In the winter, holes were cut out of the ice to obtain water. Wood for the cooking range and the barrel heater was obtained in the surrounding forest. We had no electricity, but a kerosene lamp and Coleman lantern provided light. An outhouse took care of nature's bidding in the summer and cold icy winters; one usually didn't do much reading or tarry long at 30° below zero. In the spring the winter's ice would slowly start moving in the Kispiox River. Huge chunks crashed and leaped in the air like giant daggers. The ice jammed and the river rose rapidly until the ice dam burst and allowed the water to roar down the valley.

We had sourdough starter and ate delicious sourdough pancakes and bread on a regular basis. I shot a moose and a goat and caught many salmon to help fill our larder for the long winters, as we lived off the land as much as possible. I remember one day when Scott caught a nice Dolly Varden trout in front of the cabin on the river. Scott remembers all the moose meat and peas we ate at the cabin with a certain amount of disdain, but I thought it was delicious. I never hunted again after leaving the Kispiox.

Flying lower, I couldn't locate the cabin on the Kispiox. Perhaps I wasn't supposed to find it. It is in my distant past and is not part of my present world. Kathy and I were divorced in 1971.

About twelve miles east of the cabin's location is the beautiful glacier-covered Mount Thomlinson, 8,050 feet high. Soaring low I swooped over a familiar ranch and spotted other landmarks I recognized along the banks of this tranquil, lazy river called the Kispiox.

Flying south I left the cabin on the Kispiox behind. In a time past, it was a dream realized from my early teenage years.

In the summer of 1953, my high school buddy, Jim Goerz; classmates Lee McLaughlin and Ben Mitchell, our coach, Mr. Bowdey, whom we fondly called "Chops," and his wife Bernice all went to the Olympic National Park on the Washington coast for a two-week vacation. We visited Lake Quinault Lodge and drove east of there several miles. Then we backpacked some thirteen miles into Enchanted Valley to an old lodge surrounded by many beautiful waterfalls. We saw black bear and many Roosevelt elk along the trail in the rain forest.

When Jim and I returned to Northwest Christian High School in Spokane that fall, we met secretly in the library to discuss our life's guide, a book written by Vena and Bradford Angier called *At Home in the Woods*. The book told about living off the land for ten dollars a week and about escaping civilization and living a simple self-sufficient life in the wilderness. We made plans to run away from home and live in the Canadian wilderness. I planned to steal some horses near Colville, Washington, to use as pack animals on our

Larry is watching Beavers land and take off at Omineca Air Service's seaplane base at Tchesinkut Lake in May 1964 and dreaming of becoming a bush pilot. He and his family and the Goerz family were heading north to the Kispiox Valley. Larry asked the owner how many hours he required before he would hire a pilot. He said 2,000 or 3,000 hours, but he hired Larry three years later when he had a total of 300 hours.

trek north. I didn't steal any horses, but those wonderful dreams of youth were fulfilled beyond my wildest imagination.

Jim, his beautiful wife, Mardella, and their children, Brent and Laurene, met Kathy, Scott and me in Seattle in the spring of 1964, and we crossed the border near Blaine, Washington, into Canada and became landed immigrants.

On our way up north we turned south at Burns Lake, British Columbia, and drove a few miles until Jim Goerz's trailer broke down. We were near a seaplane base on Tchesinkut Lake. I remember sitting on a grassy knoll that day, watching a white de Havilland Beaver float plane operating off Tchesinkut Lake and dreaming of becoming a bush pilot someday. When I asked the owner of Omineca Air Service at the seaplane base what his requirements were when he hired a new pilot he said, "Oh, about 2,000 to 3,000 hours." I had about 60 hours but he hired me some three years later when my hours totaled about 300. Omineca Air Service also had a base at McClure Lake, which is located a few miles south of Smithers, British Columbia.

About 80 air miles west of Smithers near Terrace, British Columbia, was an area where I felled large coastal timber in the summer of 1966. One day as I worked alone on a ridge, a piece of tree hit me on my hard hat and knocked me to the ground. As I lay dazed on the ground with a dented hard hat, a de Havilland Beaver float plane flew low overhead. I told my employer,

Colburn Ide, a tall Norwegian, that I was taking time off to get a float endorsement on my private pilot's license.

After learning to fly a float plane I went on to get my Canadian commercial pilot's license and instructor's rating early the following year. Seeing the Beaver float plane fly over that day while lying dazed on the ground helped me to change careers. It was a sign of many happy years to come, flying Beaver float planes across the north, often with my cheerful son, Scott, as copilot.

Over the years of flying in the wilderness I had some close calls. *Parade Magazine*, in a January 8, 1989 article, listed the two most dangerous occupations:

1. Timber cutters and loggers had the most dangerous blue-collar job with 129.0 deaths per 100,000.

2. Airplane pilots had the most dangerous white-color job, with 97.0 deaths per 100,000.

Approximately 29 percent of the pilots I flew with or knew in the north were killed, mostly due to bad weather.

Now, after we had followed the Bulkley River for several miles, the picturesque town of Smithers appeared beneath beautiful Hudson Bay Glacier. We landed safely and refueled the plane. Kathy and I kept our Aeronca Chief two-place airplane, CF-UVX, at the Smithers Airport in the late 1960s.

About ten miles northeast of Smithers is the Driftwood Valley where we built our beautiful log home in 1968, about a year after I began my first flying job out of nearby McClure Lake (also known as Tyee Lake) with Omineca Air Service. We had the wonderful luxury of hot running water, indoor plumbing and electricity.

I remember well Scott and his dog, Gretchen, playing together in the woods, exploring the nearby creek and discovering new worlds. Scott was a strong, healthy lad and loved the outdoor world that surrounded our home in the woods.

The Goerz family settled in Smithers. Jim built a cozy log home on acreage a few miles east of town. Jim was a tall, handsome man with a dark complexion. He guided hunters for an outfitter but his main occupation was working for the railroad.

Now, after refueling the plane and eating lunch in Smithers, we lifted off the runway at 1724, climbing on our new heading of 102°, direct to Williams Lake, British Columbia. We flew by the former seaplane base at McClure Lake and at 1806 we were passing the old seaplane base at Tchesinkut Lake off our port wing about seven miles north. Both of these bases were sold to Trans Provincial Airlines in the 1970s and later were shut down.

Soon we flew over Kenny Dam on the east end of Ootsa Lake, estimating arrival at Williams Lake Airport in one hour. This vast lake country of central British Columbia is incredible, with lakes over 100 miles long, stretching as far as my eyes could see. We touched down on runway eleven at 1937 just before dark. I caught a cab to downtown Williams Lake and ate a delicious New York steak and a fabulous salad bar for a very reasonable thirteen dollars at the Simon Frazer Hotel, and stayed at a nearby motel for thirty-five dollars. At 1130 Sunday, September 10, 1989, we departed the Williams Lake Airport on a southerly heading to Felts Field at Spokane, Washington.

The dream to fly to the distant Inuit (Eskimo) village of Tuktoyaktuk on the Arctic Ocean in the Northwest Territories of Canada, and then fly west to visit the northernmost settlement in the Yukon, the Indian village called Old Crow, is now a pleasant memory.

My roots are in the Spokane and Coeur d'Alene area and it feels so good to be coming home. Pleasant memories of the Yukon and a planned return flight to the far north next summer fill my mind as we fly toward the distant southern skies where my life's journey began.

CHAPTER 2

Adventures on the Open Road

After returning from the flight to the Arctic I completed work on a manuscript. The writing of the book represented almost three years of hard but satisfying work. It was the fulfillment of a project that began in 1971: a written record for my son, Scott, of family history and flying adventures in the wilderness. Scott was often my co-pilot while winging across the north in my favorite ship of all time, the red de Havilland Beaver CF-IBP.

The original journal record, its pages now wrinkled and yellow, began in 1971. The front cover says:

Original Journal
1971
For Scott

The following events stand out on the pages:

May 31, 1971: *First flight for Watson Lake Flying Service. IBP-Bravo-local-15 minute checkout.*

June 8, 1971: *Ft. Meyers, Florida. Flew to Toronto, Miami, Ft. Meyers. After a commercial flight and spending three days helping to get the Beaver WMH on floats airworthy, I departed on a most remarkable journey from the southeast tip of the U.S. to the Yukon Territory.*

January 6, 1972: *Winter Quarter, Bellevue Community College Big Day!! Begin attending college. This winter at school was an exciting time and met some fine people.*

June 3, 1972: *First flight of season for Watson Lake Flying Service. Circuits and bumps in Cessna 185 YIG.*

June 24, 1974: *Scott arrived for the summer. So good to have you here, son.*

July 4, 1974: *Independence Day USA. Scott is here and at present is on a fishing trip. Scott and I went to the Texaco Station and Scott landed a job at $3 hour his first job. I'm really proud and feel confident he'll do OK. 2355 bedtime.*

This old and faded journal was invaluable and formed the foundation for the beginning of a project which originally was just going to be in notebook form, but eventually became a full fledged book, *Flight of the Red Beaver*.

Most of the writing was done between 9:00 p.m. and 6:00 a.m.. as I'm a bit of a night person and had to work. It was written in longhand.

When the writing of the manuscript began, I had no idea where it was going or how it would end. *Flight of the Red Beaver* took off with a personality of its own and developed over a period of time in a most unusual way and it really has no ending.

A friend typed up the first fifty pages or so of the manuscript on a word processor and did excellent work. It was a delightful experience to read the typewritten pages and watch the north come alive in print.

Later a woman from a publishing company was hired to edit and type the manuscript but because of work conflicts it went at a snail's pace, though she did excellent work.

A literary agent in Spokane was hired to edit and his wife to type the manuscript and several chapters were completed. They did very good work, but one day the agent left Spokane quite suddenly. He had submitted samples of the manuscript and letters of inquiry to several publishing companies. One publisher requested photos and showed an interest but no contract was negotiated.

After a time, I realized publishers were not breaking down my door to

Scott completed his first solo flight at age 14 at this grass strip near Issaquah.

get the manuscript, and I decided to self-publish the book. I began contacting printing companies to get an estimate on costs and to see the quality of work they did on other books. Finally, I drew up a contract with a company in Idaho to print 2,000 copies.

On Friday, June 1, 1990, I witnessed the birth of *Flight of the Red Beaver* as it came off the press after a two-year and nine month pregnancy. It was a most joyous event and I was one happy pilot! On the front cover is a color picture of my favorite plane, the red de Havilland Beaver CF-IBP, which I was flying off the fabled South Nahanni River in the Northwest Territories.

The purpose of my life's journey now seemed at hand as I prepared to depart for Seattle and give Scott a written record of the years before he was born. Actually, this was mostly a record that covered his birth, our family's life during the first years of his life in the States, and a record of our sojourn in the far north, in which he played a large part. The emotions were unbelievable.

Scott graduated from Lake Sammamish High School, Bellevue, Washington in 1978. He was one of the top discus throwers in the state, came in first at the district meet for all of King County in 1978, and I believe he still holds the school record. In 1974 when Scott was fourteen years old, I proudly watched him solo in a glider off a grass strip at Issaquah, Washington. On his sixteenth birthday, Scott soloed in a Piper J-3 Cub at Henley Aerodrome in northern Idaho, now an amusement and theme park called Silverwood. Mom, Dad and I watched this flight.

After graduation, Scott moved to Spokane to live with me. We

Scott soloed on his 16ᵗʰ birthday in this Piper J-3 Cub at Henley Areodrame in northern Idaho on January 25, 1976.

purchased a new home in Greenacres, which is in the Spokane Valley a few miles west of Liberty Lake. After building houses for a few years, he enrolled at Washington State University and five years later graduated from the School of Architecture with a degree.

While attending Washington State University, Scott became an exchange student in Denmark and lived with a Danish family. While visiting Sweden, he told me the following story. "Dad, all the Swedish women are made out of the same mold. Out of thirty Swedish women, twenty-nine are beautiful and the other one is good-looking!" One day, he told me later, while walking down the streets of a Swedish town he saw two young Swedish women walking toward him. As he passed them he had to look up, as the twin sisters were about 6'4" tall, but they came out of that same mold and were they beautiful!

Shortly after graduating Scott married Stacy Hanson and they moved to Seattle, where he worked on commercial projects for a large architectural firm. Stacy had an excellent job working for a large developer who concentrated on shopping malls. After a few years in Seattle, Scott opened his own architectural office.

Stacy is of Scandinavian descent and she could be a top model. She certainly fits Scott's description of these beautiful Swedish women. Stacy is a trim 5'10" tall, with blond hair. Scott is a well-built 6'2" tall, good-looking man, strong as a young bull, but with an easygoing nature and a kind heart. They make a handsome couple.

On the drive to my son's home to give him a copy of the book, many emotions were racing through my being. Looking at the dark night as I drove, I felt that my life's mission would be completed once Scott was given the book.

What was there left for me to experience in life? Those years as a bush pilot were my mountain top high and there were so many other adventures of which I was privileged to be a part. Life now seemed boring! There seemed to be no more challenges, no more mountains to climb, no more new worlds — beyond the most distant mountains, the farthest horizons.

Perhaps the completion of the book, these long years writing, the large sum of money spent on the project, and finally reaching the goal left a void, an emptiness and a feeling, "Is this all there is?"

Malena Mojica, who has taught school in Mexico for many years and spent a year or so teaching school in California, has been a longtime friend and pen pal. We have never met but, through letters and phone calls, I think we know each other well. Malena has a good heart and a very deep love for nature and the history of her ancestors. Malena shared the following with me, "Larry, there are three things a man needs to do in life. Have a son, plant a tree and write a book." I'm very fortunate to have experienced these three events in my life.

Upon my arrival in Seattle, I met my son at Ivar's Salmon House on Lake Union for a salmon feed and then we drove to Scott's home. He bought champagne and we had a wonderful visit. He and Stacy owned a lovely home in the Ballard district, where many of the residents are of Scandinavian descent. My emotions ran high, but mostly I felt relief to have finally given to my son this record that had been burning a hole in my gut all these years! Scott really appreciated the book. Now it was time to see if others would be interested in the story I had told.

The first place to carry *Flight of the Red Beaver* was Northwest Map Company in downtown Spokane where the owner, Steve Mitrovich, mentioned trying Auntie's Bookstore on West Riverside. Chris O'Harra, the owner, said, "Yes," and she also carried it at another one of the book stores that she and her partner, brother-in-law Shannon Ahern, own. The Book and Game Store at the Silver Lake Mall in Coeur d'Alene, Idaho sold 450 copies at book signings during two Christmas seasons at this store.

Bob Close of Watson Lake Flying Service, Yukon, ordered a case of books and has been one of my best customers. Val Keen, at the Coach House Inn at Fort Nelson, British Columbia, placed a good-sized order. The Fireweed Book Store in Whitehorse ordered a case of books and has been a steady customer ever since. I believe they are the largest book store in the Yukon.

The following was written in my journal:

July 12: Skyway Café, Felts Field. Going to have breakfast and feel good. 1030: Gone flying. I took off from the Spokane River by Felts Field in a Cessna 185 Seaplane and flew over Newman Lake. Anne Williams, a photographer for The Spokesman-Review, *took pictures from another airplane as we flew in formation.*

A few days before, Monday, July 9, 1990, a nice article in the *Coeur d'Alene Press* came out about the book. Marv Collison, a staff writer, headlined, "Pilot flies typewriter for adventure yarn."

On Thursday, July 19, 1990, *The Spokesman Review-Chronicle* had an article about *Flight of the Red Beaver* and other books written by self-published local authors. In full color on the front page of the Empire Life section, was the picture of a Cessna 185 seaplane that I was flying over Newman Lake, Washington. The photo was taken by Anne Williams on the July 12 photo session we had over Newman Lake. The bold headline read:

FLYING SOLO In the Publishing Business.

On July 6, 1990, I was interviewed at the KXLY radio station by Alex Wood for a half-hour about the book and experiences as a bush pilot. Tim Adams, the smiling, congenial weatherman and enthusiastic student pilot, was at the station and we talked afterwards about flying. I gave him an autographed copy of my book and encouraged him to continue his flying. He later obtained his private pilot's license and we swap a few stories from time to time.

Monday, December 10, 1990, about 12:45: *I finished my twenty-minute talk. Now I can get on with my life and my next book,* Northern Flight of

Dreams.

Talked to a group of businessmen about the book and life up north. I was awake until 0500 worrying about it and was quite nervous, but gave the talk and they seemed to enjoy it. When I left and got out in the parking lot by my car, it was such a relief to have it over, that I felt like I could now do almost anything. Speaking before a group of strangers has always been a tough thing for me to do.

Went to a Swedish church yesterday with my aunts, Sue and JoAnn, for a Swedish smorgasbord dinner. It was great food.

On December 10, I sent Wilbur O'Brien two books. He flew helicopters out of Watson Lake when I was there and now, at this writing, is president of ERA Aviation in Anchorage, Alaska.

On December 12, Darell Nelson, the outfitter, called and ordered three books. Darell owns Northwest Territorial Outfitters in the Northwest Territories.

After too many years of doing too many of the same things, I wanted to feel the fresh breeze of change and experience some new adventures. After a large influx of people and a large increase in crime, perhaps it was time to find a quiet, kinder place to settle down away from the Spokane area.

It had been twenty-five years since I punched a clock or worked for someone else and I really had no inclination to change. What could I do to provide a living? After much thought, I decided to sell my home at Liberty Lake, Washington, and invest some of the profit into 5,000 copies of *Flight of the Red Beaver* books. The first printing was of poor quality and I located a printer in Spokane that appeared to do excellent work.

We agreed on a price which included new enlarged pictures, and a plastic coating on the book cover that would protect as well as create an attractive deep luster on the front cover picture of the "Red Beaver." Typographical errors would be corrected.

At the end of December, 1990, I put my house up for sale and sold it within a few weeks to a couple from Seattle. After I made a substantial deposit and signed a contract for a set price at the printing company, work began on the second revised edition of the Red Beaver book!

Near the first of February after the closing of my house, I was invited to stay with two long-time friends, Nancy Pickett and her mother Lucille McLaughlin until the books were printed. They provided me with a private room and bath in their beautiful valley home and treated me like family. The home cooking was delicious, too delicious, as I quickly put on several pounds. One day, I introduced them to my favorite Liberty Creek Trail and we had a delightful hike.

Nancy's brother, Lee, was my classmate and friend at Northwest Christian High School from 1952 to 1956. He was one of those on that special hike into Enchanted Valley in the summer of 1953. Lee was a tall, broad-shouldered, nice-looking young man with a kind spirit and good heart, who had his own horse and loved the outdoors.

Morning at McDonald's

One of my first stops most mornings is the McDonald's restaurant on North Sullivan in Veradale, Washington, in the Spokane Valley about five miles west of the Idaho border.

Friendly Mary Kinzer usually takes my order, which she knows well an apple bran muffin, medium coffee, water with no ice, and a spoon so I can dunk the apple bran muffin in the coffee. A good Swede is a good dunker!

Kaye Croyle's happy greeting, "Hi Larry, how are you?" makes me feel good and we usually chat a bit. Kaye, the hostess, has read my book and passed it on to her parents in Canada, who are familiar with the area where I flew. Her warm and friendly manner and interest in the lives of the McDonald's regulars is well-known and appreciated. Kaye speaks highly of her husband and children, and we often talk about our grandchildren.

Jill Barstow was a previous hostess, but she quit and went back to school. We have been friends for several years. Jill lived for many years on a ranch and loves the outdoors.

Sue Slippy and Jay Gentry are two of the assistant managers. I have known them for several years and we have a pleasant chat from time to time.

Chris Olney, a quiet, easy-going, friendly gentleman, is the manager. He and his wife recently moved into their custom-built dream home on the South Hill in Spokane.

Tom Burdatta is another manager who often works nights and is having a new house built on land I sold him in Greenacres in the Spokane Valley. Tom has worked here at the Sullivan McDonald's for several years and when I walk in we often visit.

Ray and Mel Brown are two retired brothers in their sixties, who I see almost every day when they come in for breakfast. They are part of the regulars and are friendly, likable gentlemen with a kind spirit. They live on some acreage nearby in the valley and we talk about the outdoors and fishing, as they have a cabin at a lake north of Spokane.

One of the regulars who, like myself, has a regular table staked out to do paperwork, is Lisa Sprank. She teaches high school and I often see her working on papers for her students. Lisa has three lovely daughters, Marissa, Holly and Brooke.

Because I spend a lot of time at this McDonald's and wrote much of *Flight of the Red Beaver* at the southeast corner booth, as well as write in my journal and read the newspapers, it has become over the years a familiar part of my life. It's a friendly place! I'm like an old dog, sea dog that is, and coming into McDonald's first thing in the morning for coffee is usually the first stop I make on my daily rounds.

On March 20, 1991, after removing the front passenger and rear seats, I put a piece of plywood that had been sanded and cut to fit on the floor of my favorite car, the blue 1978 Buick LeSabre, creating a solid platform to set the boxes of books on.

On Friday, March 23, I witnessed the second birth of *Flight of the Red Beaver* as the first of 5,000 books was launched off the press. The shiny new covers, showing the "Red Beaver" taking off the fabled Nahanni River in the Northwest Territories and the enlarged pictures within the covers, spoke of adventure!

The books were delivered to the home of my favorite aunt, JoAnn McDaniel, in the Spokane Valley, as she graciously let me keep them there until they were needed. The rest of my earthly possessions, except what I would need while traveling, were put in storage.

Adventure was in the air and my spirit soared. It was almost time to experience the freedom of the open road.

On Saturday, March 24, 1991, my blue LeSabre had a heavy payload and the back of the car rode quite low. On top of the plywood platform I'd installed were twelve cases of books. On top of the books was a four-inch foam pad inside a form-fitting sheet, covered by a blue blanket and my old blue down-filled sleeping bag, which I'd purchased from the outfitter Tommy Walker in 1967.

I have used this bag ever since as part of my survival gear while flying and to cover my bed at night. As a young boy, a blue blanket was my constant companion, so perhaps the blue sleeping bag fulfills that role, even though I'm a much bigger boy now. We have traveled thousands of miles together in the Red Beaver; it kept me warm and comfortable on cold nights in the northern wilderness over the years and continues to do so today.

The car was loaded with a suitcase, several boxes, covered clothes on hangers, tools, maps, brochures, flashlight everything that I thought I'd need for an extended trip, including four newly purchased tires. The only reason to return to Spokane would be to get more books. When I visited Scott while he was going to Washington State University's School of Architecture, he called the Buick "the Land Yacht" because of its large size. Well, it looked like a well-loaded yacht, but ready to hit the road.

My only source of income for the next year and over 50,000 miles of travel would be from the sale of my book *Flight of the Red Beaver*. The open road beckoned!

My blue Buick and I departed McDonald's Restaurant in the Spokane Valley and turned onto I-90 heading west. We stopped in downtown Spokane to check on steam that was fogging up the windows. An informed attendant at a service station said, "Your heater radiator core needs to be replaced. Just turn off your heater and you can safely drive until you can get it fixed. It won't hurt anything."

"Thanks, I think I'll get it fixed later. I want to hit the road!" I told him.

What a thrill to hit I-90 and leave Spokane behind as we drove west on course to my son's home in Ballard, located along the locks between the Puget Sound and Lake Union. Many of the residents are fishermen and their fishing boats line the several marinas by the town.

We pulled off I-90 at Ritzville and stopped at a restaurant. A second cup of coffee with some whole wheat toast gave me a spurt of energy and the desire to hit the open road. Now was the time to promote my book and perhaps I'd be fortunate enough to get a movie contract. The cover on the book sitting on my table looked great and the hard detailed work on the book was over.

It was cold in the car and I wrapped the sleeping bag around my feet. At last I was free. I could make my living with my own hands, selling books. Or at least that was the plan. Life on the road beckoned and the idea of being footloose and fancy free appealed to me. After spending the previous fifteen years in real estate, I felt burned out.

As we pull out on the open road at 1153, ash from Mount St. Helens' eruption was still very visible along the side of the road. The familiar drive heading through Moses Lake, crossing the bridge at Vantage, climbing up the rather steep hill into the foothills of the Cascade Mountain range, crossing Snoqualmie Pass at just over 3,000 feet, and driving down the west slope to nearby Seattle went smoothly.

The usual stop at Ivar's Fish Bar on Lake Union took place about 10 p.m. The smell of the alder wood smoked salmon and extra order of corn bread hit the spot. A woman and I had a nice conversation and I gave her a business card with a colored picture of the Red Beaver, the book title, and my name and address.

After dinner, I drove to Scott's and we watched Charlton Heston in "Moses." I gave Scott a copy of the latest printing and he thought it looked very good. The following morning at 0558 found me getting dressed for an early start that I hoped would prove profitable in the promotion and selling of my book.

After breakfast I drove to Edmonds to catch a ferry and drive to colorful Port Townsend, where I hoped to get some book orders from the many book and gift stores which cater to the tourist trade. However, my Buick had other ideas and chose this moment for the radiator core to give up completely. The car filled with steam and it was now necessary to replace the core. A General Motors dealership repaired the car and about 1315 we were on the ferry to Kingston, crossing Puget Sound to Port Townsend. Whitecaps, the gentle rocking of the ferry, and the constant vibration of the engine reminded me of the years on my ship, the USS Hassayampa AO-145 in the U.S. Navy. The snow-capped peaks of the westerly Olympic Mountains rose above the sound with some of the tops in the clouds. We (my Buick and I) arrived at Port Townsend in mid-afternoon and I walked around town trying to promote and sell books. None of the owners or buyers seemed to be in the stores that day and no orders or sales were made there.

By evening I was back at the dock waiting for a ferry boat to Seattle. It had been a long and somewhat frustrating day, but the car was fixed and the country was spectacular. Back at Scott's, I felt much better after a shower and it was good to spend time with him. The following morning my eyes were burning and telling me to get more sleep.

After I stopped and showed my book at the University Book Store, they said they would order some books and a woman at their Bellevue store also agreed to place an order later. I stopped at Bob Monroe's, the owner of

Larry served onboard the USS Hassayampa AO-145, an oil tanker, from1956-1958, visiting Japan, Philippines, New Zealand and Hong Kong.

Kenmore Air Harbor, a seaplane base, and gave Bob an autographed copy of my book. Bob specialized in rebuilding Beavers and is well known around the country for the work his company does. He had one of his employees make out a check for ten books.

The next morning after a restful sleep, we left Scott's with frost on the windows, but the morning was beautiful. We delivered twelve books to the Boeing Museum of Flight, and at 1:45 p.m. we were on the road to Vancouver, British Columbia, on our promotional tour.

At 1547 we were at Blaine, Washington, a border crossing into British Columbia. It was 27 years earlier when Scott, Kathy and I crossed here with Jim Goerz and his family. I kissed the ground just a little north of here on the Canadian side when we crossed and became landed immigrants, fulfilling our boyhood dreams. We were all young then. Scott was 4 years old, Kathy was 24 and I was 26. The wings of time have more than doubled my years since then.

It was two city blocks to the bright white Peace Arch, with the American and Canadian flags flying high. The inscription by the Peace Arch reads:

Children of a common mother
1814 OPEN 100 YEARS 1914

The list of the provinces and the territories read:

British Columbia	*New Brunswick*
Alberta	*Nova Scotia*
Saskatchewan	*Prince Edward Island*
Manitoba	*Newfoundland*
Ontario	*Yukon Territory*
Quebec	*Northwest Territory*

The car in front of me had a Canadian license plate, #SPP 165, proudly proclaiming: "Beautiful British Columbia."

We crossed the border about 4 p.m. but because of the books we had to turn back and cross farther east at the truck crossing. We crossed at the commercial crossing, but I had to leave the books on the U.S. side because of a 7 percent new tax they charged on any books brought into Canada, even if they didn't sell. The previous year there had been no tax.

After I was told about the seven percent Canadian tax on books, I left my books at Ernie Henken's Used Car Lot at 2001 James St. in Bellingham, Washington. I met Ernie and his wife at a restaurant in Bellingham and happened to mention my plight and he said "Leave your books here and pick them up tomorrow." What a nice couple to befriend a complete stranger. They used to take their boat up to Rivers Inlet along the British Columbia coast to fish for large King Salmon and I told them I had flown fishermen there in a float plane from McClure Lake near Smithers, British Columbia. During my journeys across the country I met other quality people like the Henkens, kind and helpful. People are great for the most part, although we all have our bad days!

I stayed at the Best Western Motel by the Vancouver Airport. The following day, Friday, I left some information at the Vancouver Airport for Bomber Joe's Aviation Book Store, which was closed. I also left a book with a man who said he would drop it off the next day at the book store. As a result of this effort, I have been given regular orders from Bomber Joe's Book Store for over a year. Promoting a book, I was learning, is a hard, time-consuming job.

Leaving Canada we went south through the Seattle area, and overnighted at the Jantzen Beach Red Lion Motor Inn in Portland, Oregon. Driving on through Oregon I spent a night in Santa Barbara, California, where I dropped off six books at Fess Parker's Red Lion Inn. Fess Parker, the movie star, was on vacation, but he wrote me a nice handwritten letter later,

Larry's neighbor Bill Love of Love Brothers and Lee Outfitters, Fred Bear of Bear Bows, and Larry's childhood hero Fess Parker, who played Davy Crockett and Daniel Boone on television, are shown here on a hunting trip near Stevens Lake in B.C. Fess shot a grizzly bear near this Stevens Lake cabin (see inset), where this world record grizzly was shot with a bow and arrow by Rex Hancock, a dentist from the southern states that Larry flew in and out.

thanking me for the books and telling me to say hello to the people up North. In the letter he wrote, "My son recently obtained his commercial pilot's license and enjoyed your book."

My neighbor in the Kispiox Valley, Bill Love, guided Fess and Fred Bear, the maker of the Bear Bow, on a grizzly bear hunt at the headwaters of the Kispiox River near Stevens Lake. I have a picture of Bill Love, Fred Bear, and Fess Parker in *Flight of the Red Beaver*. Fess shot a bear on that hunt in the same area where I flew out the world record grizzly bear taken with a bow in the late 1960s. He had been a boyhood hero of mine when he played Davy Crockett and Daniel Boone in the 1950s and inspired me to live in the wilderness someday.

On Sunday, April 7, 1991, I was autographing books under the old London Bridge in Lake Havasu, Arizona. The London Bridge, brought over from England and reassembled stone by stone, is the second largest tourist attraction in Arizona. On the front page of that day's local paper was the headline, "Answering the Wild Blue's Call," and a brief story about my book and life in the north.

After leaving Arizona, I drove through Utah, Montana, and Idaho, and back to Washington. In the middle of April I was back in the Seattle area, where I wrote in my journal:

1851: *Ivar's on the Waterfront (Puget Sound, downtown Seattle). Have a book displayed. Ate salmon & chips and coffee. Bright sunshine glistens on the water, too bright to stare at long, like looking at the sun.*

Seagulls squawking and a pigeon eating a french fry nearby inside the enclosure. The seagulls are flying west of the glass, a few feet above the water in a counterclockwise circle, as people feed them scraps. Traffic noises in the background roar, but it feels good at this time of my life.

I have an appointment to see Judy Hunt of the Seattle Post-Intelligencer *newspaper at 1030 tomorrow and she may do an article on my book, sounds encouraging.*

Also an appointment with Helen Ibach of Pacific Pipeline, as I have decided to put my book there so it can be distributed.

Interesting people. Looks like a group of Indians at a nearby table, Haida Indians? One sure looks the part, with long hair to his waist and a Manchu mustache. The woman next to him has long dark brown hair and another male has a mustache; a small child sits between them.

A green four-wheel horse-drawn buggy is heading south by the window on the east side, down Alaska Way. Saw one gentleman with a long white beard. He looked like a Viking.

When I was a boy and came here with my parents, we walked along the waterfront and watched the large ships docked on the various piers along Alaska Way. It was an awesome sight to see the size of the ships and to imagine where they came from and where they were bound.

Now I have memories of those early years and of the two years when I was on an oil tanker, the USS Hassayampa, in the north and south Pacific. I have indeed been most fortunate to have had life experiences in the Far East and up in the far northern wilderness.

The sun's about 10 degrees above the horizon, and sinking quickly. It's amazing that once the sun touches the horizon, it's only a few minutes before it disappears and darkness falls on the earth. I'm so fortunate to be here, recording the ending of another day, for my health and for God's wonderful creation that I see and behold. In the far west rise the magnificent Olympic Mountains that I know well.

Another ferry is coming in and a ship anchored in the distance beyond the ferry sits peacefully.

Women talking at a table across the room, talking with their hands as well as their mouths. Women seem to love animated lengthy talks with each other.

The waterfront is alive, a busy living place. The water on the Puget Sound 50 feet west of me is a medium blue with a bit of a ripple. A ferry is crossing northwest across the sound beneath a cloud that is shaped like a Viking holding a club or maybe it's a mother with flowing hair, holding a child.

Talked to the driver of a black limousine who just left. He had the limo parked illegally out front. He is just driving south, away from Ivar's. He took his clam chowder and left.

A black couple is sitting next to me now; and across the aisle two very large ladies are enjoying the fish and clam chowder.

I love this place, memories of long ago, when I was a young boy, surface and I remember the old Ivar's here. Eating dinner here was a big event when my family came over.

A child's cry. Jonathan Livingston Seagull, or one of his kin, is soaring and lands on the rooftop of Ivar's, as the rest of the flock looks on in a rather superior manner. They are part of the flock that do the expected, live the normal life, the boring, normal part of society that all too many are part of.

The sun has set behind Ivar's roof top, behind the neon sign that glows red and blue. My life is rather simple right now: a car, books to sell for living expenses and completing my second book: Northern Flight of Dreams: A Journey through Time.

Maybe I'll go to the Olympics, hike to Enchanted Valley and take pictures.

An Oriental woman with a male companion sits across the aisle. I have an attraction for Orientals.

Am on my second cup of coffee. Talked briefly to a school teacher from Griffon College. So many places to sell my book, so many people. What an opportunity, Larry!

Darkness is descending over the inland ocean waters of Puget Sound. The sky is more pink in color with a dark purple touching the mountains.

8:22 p.m. or 2022 Pilot Time ...

Traffic noises as well as human sounds are quieting down as darkness descends.

Time to head out. Light blinking across the waters of the sound. Time to go, Larry. The mood of darkness descends.

An older gentleman is sitting across the aisle, white hair, looks Scandinavian, dipping his spoon in Ivar's clam chowder.

The ferry lights of an oncoming ferry make it look like a floating building as it approaches.

The appointment with Judy Hunt of the *Seattle Post-Intelligencer*, a major Seattle paper, went well. We had a friendly talk and it appeared that she was going to do a story on my book and life! GREAT!

The appointment with Helen Ibach went well and she agreed to carry my books at a 52% discount off the retail price, which we put at $15.95. The book would go into their catalog and they service 2,000 stores in the West and Canada. Many stores like Waldenbooks and B. Dalton who would only order through wholesalers and wouldn't let me sell direct to them are serviced by Pacific Pipeline. This opened a whole new market to me.

I also contacted Jim French's office. He has a very popular radio talk show in the Seattle area on KIRO Radio. Jim wasn't in, but I talked to a woman who said it sounded like something they might like to do and that she would pass the information on to Mr. French.

At last things were beginning to come together for me. Self publishing, I have learned, means self-promoting. The newspapers that ran articles about my book and the radio talk show hosts that interviewed me about the book and life as a bush pilot all were contacted by me. Self-promotion was a time-consuming job and much hard work over a long period was required to make *Flight of the Red Beaver* FLY! But it was well worth the effort and I have no regrets.

Often in life when it seems that I have hit a brick wall, with no way around or over, persistence finally wins out and the path opens. During the past several years I have also learned that what seem to be negative happenings in my life have invariably turned out to be positive things in life's journey. So often just trying a little longer and not giving up is all it takes and usually the solution or answer is much closer than imagined.

Now when a negative thing happens I just know it's really going to be a positive event in my life, and I'm able to relax a bit, confident that it's truly going to be OK!

When *Flight of the Red Beaver* was printed I wasn't sure if the public, or even friends, would like my book. The main purpose was to leave a record for my son, Scott, and I felt he would appreciate it. The feedback from people who read the book was very positive and I felt that with the proper promotion and getting the word out, it would sell well. I didn't know many of the people who wrote letters and phoned me after reading my book, but it was marvelous to hear from each of them.

I contacted Patty Morris, the district manager of Waldenbooks at South Center Shopping Mall. She was interested in the book and eventually carried it, ordering through Pacific Pipeline. It was also carried by three other Waldenbooks in the Seattle area and Alaska, as well as many other bookstores in the Seattle and surrounding communities.

(From left to right) Jim Goerz, Ben Mitchell, Larry, Lee McLaughlin, Mr. Bowdey (Chops) and his dog hiking into Enchanted Valley in Olympic National Park in the summer of 1953.

Things were opening up for the Red Beaver!
The following was written in my journal:

April 19, 1991: *Am on a ferry going to Victoria, British Columbia.*

0614: *The steady vibration of the Kingston Ferry reminds me again of the ship I was on in the Pacific. Fog, just getting light, a new day. I'm taking 14 books with me and going to the office of the magazine Beautiful B.C. Talking to a couple of gentlemen.*

0804: *Port Angeles. Standing in line to board the Black Ball Ferry.*

0810: *On board the ferry, near the bow on the observation deck. The sun is burning through the fog with visibility about one mile. The road to the ferry was quite foggy a good part of the way.*

Scott and I stayed up until 0100 and I was up at 0500, not much sleep. I feel this trip is necessary to get my book in Victoria B.C. and the rest of Canada. The bow is similar to my ship, the USS Hassayampa AO-145.

0819: *The whistle of the ship (ferry) must indicate we will soon be underway.*

0838: *Fog. Swells rocking the ferry. Fog horn is blowing. Sitting next to a gentleman from Edmonton who's originally from Egypt.*

0927: *Thick fog continues, but eventually Victoria appears. Looking across the bay I can see three twin-engine Otters (airplanes).*

My trip to Victoria, B.C., was successful. I left some books at the largest book store there, Munro's Bookstore. I thought that Beautiful B.C. was going to order quite a few, and a woman named Jennifer was supposed to contact me; however, they never contacted me, and I wondered if they didn't care for the hunting stories.

After my book promotions were accomplished, I spent a short time enjoying Victoria before catching the ferry for the return trip to Port Angeles. There were many groups of Asians speaking their own language in Victoria. Large numbers of wealthy Asians are flocking to the Vancouver-Victoria area and the price of real estate has increased sharply.

1637: *We're near the center of the strait between Victoria and Port Angeles and a hazy sun shines brightly. The Olympics, in all their snow-capped majesty, rise out of the water ahead and south of our bow. The ship was taking a rather zigzag course, but it's now holding steady as she goes. There are a few ships about, a tanker crossed our bow from west to east several minutes ago and a freighter is passing our starboard, about a mile west. There are quite a few older retired people, some young couples with children and a few single ladies. I've been talking to a couple from Arkansas sitting next to me.*

1840: *Beautiful Crescent Lake Mr and Mrs. Bowdey took us here in 1953. That was my first visit here. Where does time go? We were kids then, Jim, Lee, Ben and I. Mr. Bowdey, our high school coach, was a Christian man I deeply admired.*

Mallard hen about 8 feet away and another 15 or so mallard ducks close by. The quiet lapping waters bring peace to my soul. Thank you God. The moss covers the rock I sit on and the snow covered peaks come steeply down, forming a very deep lake. I'm so fortunate. The rock is quite warm, even though the sun has set behind a mountain across the lake.

It's so beautiful and yet so sad that I can't share this again with Mr. and Mrs. Bowdey, Ben, Lee and Jim. It can never be again in this life. Mr. Bowdey passed away a few years ago and one of my former classmates is in a wheelchair.

Glaciers covered this valley thousands of years ago. Lake Crescent is 600 feet deep.

CHAPTER 3

Olympic Rain Forest

I drove on into the night. At 2052, I stopped at the town of Forks for a hamburger, and then continued on to Lake Quinault Lodge.

The first time I visited this old rustic lodge was with my high school buddy Jim Goerz, when we were fifteen years old, in 1953. My son, Scott, came here with me when he was fourteen years old, and he introduced his wife Stacy to this special place a few years ago. I wrote in my journal:

I'm sitting on a wicker chair at the Lake Quinault Lodge. My book Flight of the Red Beaver *sits on a table made from a five-foot slice of a large log. About twenty feet from my chair, the fire crackles quietly as the burnt-up logs glow red. A couple next to me is playing cards, as are three other couples at another table. Another couple just walked up to the fireplace and are looking at some totem pole designs on a flat board hanging down from the mantle. Maybe I can get my book displayed in the gift shop!*

April 20, 1991, Saturday, 1220: *Lake Quinault Lodge. Lunch in the dining room. From the west a breeze farther out on the lake causes slight ripples, but there is a calm spot in front of the lodge.*

Talked to the waitress and she knows Watson Lake. Sold a book to a couple from Chillawack, British Columbia, two to a lady at the next table, one to a man from New Zealand. A woman from Seattle bought two books and a waitress bought one. Six books sold so far at lunch very

This is Lake Quinault Lodge, which is located about 30 miles east of the Pacific Ocean in the Olympic National Forest in Washington state.

profitable lunch.

1550: *I drove thirty miles to the ocean. I'm standing on a steep bank overlooking a stony beach and watching the breakers come in from the Pacific.*

1648: *Klaloch Lodge Coffee Shop. Looking west out the dining room picture windows, endless breakers of the vast Pacific continue to roll in. The brightness of the sun on the whitecaps has increased as the sun dips lower toward the horizon. A beachcomber walks along the ocean about a quarter of a mile away.*

Nearby, log cabin rentals sit on a bluff overlooking the ocean. Tasted the salt water yep, salty! Sitting on a shiny log on the ocean beach close to the roar of the waves. Met a woman from Vancouver walking on the beach. She's walking down the beach now on a southerly heading. What a lovely day.

1914: *Back to Lake Quinault. Float plane just took off.*

1940: *Starting up a trail into the rain forest about a mile west of the lodge. Rich green fern, white flowers, huge tall trees, moss on the bushes along the trail hangs down, like in the bayous of the deep South.*

(Left picture) Jim Goerz, Lee McLaughlin, Larry and Benny Mitchell catching smelt in the Pacific Ocean and (right) cleaning their limit in clams.

The evening air is sweet with the smell of this dense, rich rain forest. I stop and breathe deep and look at a tall, straight tree about ten feet across the base. Looking down I can see a beautiful crystal-clear stream that circles around a rock on both sides and drops several feet, making a white foamy color and a light roaring sound. The pool below the falls swirls in a clockwise motion.

A sign along the trail reads:

RAIN FOREST: The rain forest is much more than just the presence of certain plants. It's a living, dying, complete community of plants and animals, elk browsing through the forest shadows, salmon jumping waterfalls and moss and seedlings growing on decaying logs. This and much more make up the Olympic Rain Forest.

The stream is so pure that the rocks on the bottom are easily seen in the fading twilight. Giant Sitka Spruce, Hemlock, Douglas Fir and Western Red Cedar surround me in a magnificent and comforting way. The half moon can be seen touching the top of a nearby tree.

2000: I'm Sitting in the middle of a fallen old giant that spans a gorge. The sound of birds, the mosquitos trying to take a part of me and the rush of a nearby waterfall on the friendly stream are my companions.

I love the desert, as I think of Lake Havasu a few weeks ago, but really I am most at home here in this rain forest, the Pacific Northwest area of lakes, ocean, rivers and mountains. This is my home, this is my land, this is where my body was born and where it hopefully will be laid to rest. It's in my bones, my flesh, my soul. I love this country with a deep and passionate love.

Better get up from my friendly fallen giant and continue up the trail before it gets darker. Thank you God for this moment. The mosquitos are certainly large like the forest, they grow big!

A sign reads: "Quinault Giants: The largest trees are Douglas Fir. They are nearly 500 years old and 300 feet high. There is enough timber growing here in a single acre (approximately the size of a football field) to build 40 average houses."

Sitting on another fallen, but smaller giant, a bit of Quinault Lake can be seen through the trees.

April 21, 1991, Sunday: *Olympic National Park trip, clear-cut, overcast, windows are wet with dew and fog is just above the tree tops.*

0735: *Lying in my bed (the foam on top of my books), inside my blue down-filled sleeping bag. It's my link with the past; I often slept in it while making my bed in the Beaver. At night the waves on a wilderness lake would lap against the floats as they rocked me to sleep.*

I'm in the middle of a clear-cut, parked about 200 yards from Highway 101 some ten miles south of Lake Quinault Lodge. I slept well.

0950: *At the restaurant in Lake Quinault Lodge. The annual rainfall here is about 145 inches, according to a sign near a totem pole in back of the lodge.*

Monday, April 22, 1991: *I drove back to Spokane yesterday.*

1349: *Sitting in McLaughlin's living room waiting for a phone call, probably from Seattle. It came in a bit ago. They said they would call again in ten minutes. Doing laundry. Judy Hunt, Seattle P.I., wanted to know if there was any truth in the old saying: "There are old pilots and there are bold pilots, but no old bold pilots." Talked to Judy Hunt again a bit later as she wanted some more info about the short flying season. I scheduled the newspaper article and the radio talk show for Friday, April 26, 1991. This gained us some free advertising for the special Seaplane weekend and for my autograph session at the Boeing Field Museum of Flight the following day. It worked great!*

Tuesday, April 23, 1991

1614: *Sitting in a restaurant in Issaquah and reading the* Seattle Times *paper. Going to make phone calls shortly and call all the bookstores I can. Tomorrow they take my mug shot at Kenmore Aviation for the* Seattle Post-Intelligencer *newspaper article on my book. It will come out on Friday.*

2200: *At Ballard. Scott's house is shutting down and it's quiet. Scott and Stacy have gone to bed.*

I met the photographer for the *Seattle Post-Intelligencer* newspaper at Kenmore Aviation and he took several photos of me standing beside a Cessna 185 float plane. It went well.

I dropped off a carload of books at Pacific Pipeline, a book wholesaler and distributor. Then I started contacting bookstores in the Seattle and Tacoma area to let them know about my book. The ones I didn't visit personally, phoned. I told them about the *Seattle Post-Intelligencer's* article that would come out in the Friday, April 26, 1991, edition, and the KIRO radio talk show interview the same day.

With these calls to as many bookstores in the area as I could locate, I was able to create a demand and awareness for my book and give the bookstores a few days lead time to enable them to order from Pacific Pipeline before the news blitz hit. It worked and orders started rolling in! You can't be afraid to "toot your own horn" when promoting your book!

April 26, 1991

0824: At Scott's home in Ballard. In just under two hours I'm scheduled to be on Jim French's KIRO radio talk show. Scott is getting ready to go back to his office. He cranked away until 0400 this morning trying to get a design job finished that is scheduled for completion.

The birds are singing and I feel a quietness within about the talk show, though I must be honest, I also feel some butterflies, like when I was going for a check ride in an airplane I hadn't flown, or for a check ride examination for a pilot's license or rating. So, it's a normal reaction, I guess.

The quietness and peace I feel here at Scott and Stacy's home is refreshing and soothing. Many memories are in Flight of the Red Beaver. *Many lives that touched mine are recorded in print as are stories about that wonderful land called the Yukon.*

1008: *Sitting in KIRO radio's waiting room-lobby. The waiting will soon be over and I'll have the privilege of telling the story about* Flight of the Red Beaver. *It's almost time, Larry. Give it a go, do your best, talk plainly and don't trail off at the end of your sentences.*

The talk show went okay, but was short. I did mention the planned autograph session at the Boeing Museum of Flight at Boeing Field on Saturday.

After the show I purchased the *Seattle Post-Intelligencer* paper and there was a good picture of me standing on the left float of a Cessna 185 with my right hand on the cowling. The picture and the article was on the top half of the living section on D9. The heading in bold print said: "Flying the Unfriendly Skies: Author recounts the dangerous ups and downs of a bush pilot" right above "Seaplane Weekend Events Calendar."

It was a good article; I made hand-out copies to give to bookstores and put one in a large picture frame with other newspaper articles to display when I was autographing books.

This weekend was most unusual and exciting. It was a special seaplane weekend event at the Museum of Flight and many notable pilots were there. Tom Casey, who recently completed the first solo seaplane flight around the world, gave an interesting slide presentation of his epic flight, part of which

I was privileged to see. Greg Monroe of Kenmore Air Harbor gave a slide presentation on seaplane flying.

Before my autograph session began Saturday at the museum, Peggy McCaully, the coordinator of the seaplane weekend event and a pilot, escorted me upstairs to the Barnstormers Lounge. I met and shared some stories of the far north with Noel Merrill Wien, son of the famous pioneer Alaska bush pilot Noel Wien, who is a hero of mine. Noel Wien, Jr. is a seasoned bush pilot in his own right, as well as an airline pilot. Tom Casey was there and shared his experience of making an emergency landing in the ocean when his engine quit. It was scary!

I met Everett Riggs, an interesting and friendly gentleman from Sitka, Alaska, who recently retired from Alaska Airlines, and his son, Eugene Riggs, who is a pilot for Alaska. Eugene lives in a nearby airpark, next door to Noel Wien, Jr., and they both keep their Grunman Widgens (amphibian airplanes) there. Eugene's brother Butch also flies for Alaska. We all sat around in the Barnstormers Lounge, sharing flying stories of the North. Any time pilots get together the stories begin to fly and we became one, thanks to our love of flying. These men from Alaska were warm and friendly, like the northern people I knew and lived with in the Yukon.

I began autographing my book at 1100 Saturday at the Museum of Flight and met many fellow float plane pilots and autographed about 60 books. My high school buddy, Lee McLaughlin, stopped by and introduced me to his grandson, Jeff, and we had a good visit.

One thing I remember about tall, broad-shouldered Lee from our high school days was his good heart and kindly manner. After thirty-five years we were reunited by my a book. I spent a night with Lee and his wife Kathy at their home in Federal Way south of Seattle. He was the same open, kind-hearted person I knew in high school.

Lee and I had shared one high school event that stood out above all the others: that wonderful two-week backpacking and camping trip to Olympic National Park.

We drove in the Bowdey's station wagon to Hurricane Ridge near Port Angeles, where we posed for pictures next to a deep snowbank. Most of our time was spent backpacking in the rain forest and camping along Ocean Beaches. I remember sharing the trail with Lee to beautiful Enchanted Valley, deep in the rain forest. While camping on the Pacific Ocean we dug our limit of clams. After they came out of the frying pan they had the same chewy texture as a rubber tire. I've never eaten a clam since. We got soaked as we ran out in the surf in our clothes to catch delicious smelt with nets attached to long poles.

We laughed, swapped tales, and created wonderful stories to pass down to our children's children. We listened as Mr. Bowdey led devotions and we prayed together under a canopy of giant trees, beside a rushing stream. Mr. Bowdey was a devoted Christian man I admired. He cared deeply about our lives and spent a lot of time with us over several years.

In 1990 I contacted Mrs. Bowdey by phone and we had a nice visit. She told me Mr. Bowdey had died after a long illness and that it was a blessing because he had suffered for so long. I thanked her for that wonderful trip and told her how it had shaped my life, eventually leading me to the far North. Mrs. Bowdey said that trip to the Olympics was the highlight of her life and of Mr. Bowdey's while they were teachers at Northwest Christian High School. Later she wrote to me to say she enjoyed the book.

Because Mr. and Mrs. Bowdey were kind enough to share the Olympic Rain Forest and nearby ocean beaches, I was able to introduce this beauty to my son when he was fourteen years old. We return from time to time to the Olympics to renew our spirits.

CHAPTER 4

Harrison, Lake Coeur d'Alene, and the Open Road

It was Friday July 26, 1991, as the dance band played "Pretty Woman" at the Harrison Marina in Northern Idaho. Lake Coeur d'Alene glimmered dark blue, the sun had set, and lights flickered across the lake from Grandpa's old cabin just west of Spokane Point. I found the music too loud so I took a walk by the lake.

It was the weekend of the Harrison Centennial Celebration and I felt it would be fun to spend time in my favorite small town and, if I got lucky, sell some books. I set up my autographing table early that day and sold enough books to pay expenses plus a bit more.   Sunday morning I set up my booth again and prepared for another day of book signing. At mid-morning a parade marched down Main Street. It was a good parade with many children participating. Book sales were much better than the previous day and I had some extra money jingling in my pockets at day's end.

A young man at a neighboring booth invited me to his log home for dinner. Dennis and Marcia Liming fixed a great chicken dinner in their charming log house that sits on top of the bluff overlooking Harrison and we had a nice visit. A few hours later, I was driving north toward Coeur d'Alene.

Friday, August 2, found me in the city park of Colville, Washington, for the Colville Rendezvous, which lasted for three days. It's a touch of the Old West and a time for the locals and lots of visitors to have a good time and relive a bit of the past.

It was primarily an arts and craft show and people at adjoining booths had carved wooden toys, arrowheads (some were being made while the crowd watched), and carvings. Others had crafted items on display and for sale. Because I wrote the book, published it, and took most of the pictures, the organizers let me in, figuring it was a genuine handcrafted item.

The following morning I sold more books at the Colville Rendezvous. A country and Western band played, and I talked to people about the North and swapped a few tales with fellow pilots.

That night I drove to Chewelah, Washington, about twenty miles south, and slept in the Buick in the city park.

The following morning I woke up around 0730 and drove to a nearby restaurant. Three couples from Spokane were there cutting up. They were going golfing at the Chewelah golf course north of town near the airport. Their banter back and forth kept me in stitches and finally we began visiting. Two of the attractive women sat next to me with their arms around my neck, while another took a photo of them next to a real live author.

By 1024, I was set up for another autograph session at the Rendezvous. At 1114 I met a neat woman by the name of Linda Spurling, who purchased the first book of the day. This great-looking outdoorsy woman was a cowgirl and an outfitter. Her slim figure and young outlook were much younger than her sixty-nine years. Later she came back and purchased two more books. She kept two books for herself and had me autograph another one for her friend, Grace Rice, who wrote a book called Buckaroo Girl that told about Grace's life as a bronc buster and cattle ranch owner. Meeting people like Linda Spurling who have the guts to follow and live their dreams was a rewarding experience as I traveled the country. We corresponded after the Rendezvous had long since ended.

On August 10, I drove to the home of my good friend Florence Farber. Florence is a widow and retired school teacher. Her home has a commanding view of Harrison, Lake Coeur d'Alene, the Coeur d'Alene River, and Anderson Lake. At dusk seventeen elk and a dozen deer were feeding on her alfalfa field about one-half mile east of her house.

Her place is a refuge from civilization for me, and after spending a few hours hiking and talking, I always feel at peace. Florence taught school in Alaska, so she knows the North and we have much in common. On our first hike together we walked below her 30-acre place along the State of Idaho's wildlife preserve just below her house. It was once a part of the 640-acre section that she and her husband owned.

Recently Florence visited Turkey, and before that she took a trip to her ancestral country of Poland. At this writing she is in Pennsylvania as a nanny for a small child. She felt a need to get away for a year or so, but her heart is in her beautiful home above the lake.

In life's journey, it's the Florences of the world who give life a special meaning and a special quality. Florence is one of a kind and my good friend!

Whenever I visit Harrison, my mind drifts back to those happy boyhood days with my grandfather on Lake Coeur d'Alene. Grandfather Rydblom and I would often tie up a boat to some pilings in the lake near the mouth of the Coeur d'Alene River and catch a bucket full of tasty perch. Sometimes at night I'd catch big crappies on a wet fly at the Harrison Public Dock under a bright light.

Across the lake by Doc Taylor's old floathouse, we often caught Grandpa's favorite fish, the beautiful, fighting cutthroat trout. One day he yelled out, "Here fishy, fishy!" above the roar of the motor and caught a nice cutthroat close to the boathouse.

We were close, Grandpa and I. The lake was our fortress. For Grandpa, it was an escape from his job as a lineman and phone installer for the Ma Bell Telephone Company and domestic life. For me, it was an escape from school and the adult world that was always trying to tell me what to do. I developed a deep love for nature and the great outdoors at the lake cabin Grandpa built shortly after World War II. He treated me with kindness and let me have the freedom of the lake by myself or with his dog Butch in a small duck boat powered by an old three-horsepower Johnson outboard the kind you had to start by wrapping a rope around the top and giving it a good hard yank.

Grandpa was a handsome, lean Swede, about 6'3" tall, warm-hearted and generous to a fault. He was called Bill by his friends and he had many. Grandpa wore a pair of black baggy trousers hooked to a pair of suspenders, an old hat with a 360° brim, a pair of work boots over gray socks, a brown or gray work shirt, and next to his skin 365 days a year, a pair of long johns. An original, one-of-a-kind Swede from the old country, he was fiercely proud of being a United States citizen an American. He told me to remember the Fourth of July and to fly the flag.

Life at the cabin was the best world I knew as a kid and it was the happiest period of my early boyhood years. Later I shared some of that with my son, Scott.

Grandpa was an early riser, and for breakfast he would fry a pound of bacon. My job was to make the toast, but no matter how closely I watched it always burned. But breakfast at the cabin was always delicious.

Grandpa was an excellent fisherman and had a large assortment of poles, reels, leaded lines, unleaded lines, and of course several tackle boxes of his favorite cutthroat lures. He taught me how to clean a trout quickly and how to tie a line. But the thing I remember most is that he gave me the freedom to develop on my own in that beautiful outdoor setting at Lake Coeur d'Alene.

Northeast of Harrison is a state wildlife refuge that is mostly wetlands. Often I've counted a dozen or more blue heron, hundreds of Canada geese, ducks and occasionally a swan. The area between Harrison and St. Maries has perhaps the largest concentration of osprey in the world.

I've made several flights, some in a float plane around the Harrison area over the years. Several years ago, Scott and I flew a Cessna 185 float plane from Newman Lake to Liberty Lake. Because Liberty Lake is fairly small and surrounded by trees and mountains, I left Scott there while the Liberty Lake County Park Ranger, Dan Miller, and his wife flew with me to Harrison in the float plane. I wanted to keep the airplane as light as possible so we could get out of the water quickly in order to clear the trees at the edge of the lake. It was their first visit to this unique town.

In the spring of 1976 Bill Brooks, who owns and operates Brooks Seaplane Base at the town of Coeur d'Alene, gave me a few hours of dual instruction in one of his Cessna 185 float planes. We flew up the Coeur d'Alene River several miles and landed on one of the lakes that empty into the river just east of Harrison. I think it was called Black Lake. A week later we flew a group of fishermen from New York off Lake Coeur d'Alene to beautiful Fortress Lake in the Canadian Rockies in British Columbia. We caught many two-pound to three-pound Eastern brook trout. I was following Bill's Cessna 185 when we went through a snowstorm in the Rockies. He warned me by radio, "Don't take the valley that turns right; it ends in a box canyon." I remember with fondness the crystal clear lake surrounded by the majestic Rocky Mountains.

Bill Brooks has operated Brooks Seaplane Base since the 1940s, and I remember watching him fly off the lake as a boy. He started the flying service in 1946, operating Taylor Crafts, Piper J-3 Cubs, a Super Cub, Stinson 165, and a Sea Bee. Later, he operated Cessna 180s, 185s, a Beaver and a Cessna 206 off the lake.

Bill was a lieutenant J.G. in the U.S. Navy and an instrument instructor in an observation plane called the Sikorsky OSZU from 1940 to 1943. From 1943 to 1945, he flew a huge Sikorsky VS-44 in Africa for American Export Airline (AEA). Only three of these huge four-engine flying boats, which had a range of 6,000 miles, were made. Bill and other naval pilots with flying boat experience were released from the Navy to fly these ships. Bill flew one called Excambian, which is the only survivor; it is now in the New England Air Museum in Windsor Locks, Connecticut.

A few years ago Bill bought a rebuilt de Havilland Beaver on floats and his son Grant let me fly it for a few minutes while on a flight with tourists over Lake Coeur d'Alene. I often visit Bill and Grant Brooks, swap a few tales and watch the float planes take off and land.

After leaving Harrison and the Spokane area, I headed south on the open road. During the months of September, October, and most of November of 1991, I traveled across the Western states.

On September 6, 1991 I was driving west on Highway 42 to the Oregon Coast and noticed a sign pointing to "Remote." I decided to check it out.

I wrote the following in my journal:

Arrived at Remote, a neat place from the past. It is on a side paved road that makes a loop off the highway. The store is the only building except the old house next door. Finished the roll of film while taking photos of Maude Masters at Remote. She purchased the post office and store from her sister in 1967. They moved into a house there in 1913, and her father, L. B. Jenning, built the store in 1924. Maude was born some time after they moved to Remote. She wouldn't give her age. Sign on top of the store reads, Remote, Oregon 97468. Some young loggers came in the store to pay their bills and charge some more groceries. They had black jeans cut off above the boots to keep from getting snagged in the woods, suspenders and logging boots. They bought some hot sausages in a vinegar jar and walked out the door eating their treat.

Maude closed the post office last October. She said the Postal Service didn't like her wearing sweat shirts and casual clothes, so she figured they were getting too fussy. It was a grand experience meeting her and it makes me chuckle. What a beautiful person this independent woman from Oregon is a treasure!

I continued down the road and to Bandon, Oregon, and rented a room. After dinner of red snapper, I walked through the fresh night air to the nearby beach and wrote the following in my journal:

Walking along Bandon Beach, the roar of the ocean is interspersed by the sound of a fog horn at the nearby lighthouse. The rock formations are fantastic, some jagged, some round; the sound of seagulls, the clear salt air, the mist from the heavy fog all contribute to a wonderful day.

As I stood on a rock ledge above a deep, dark pool, I thought of a killer shark, and just then water washed up around my feet with a loud roar and my heart did some flip-flops as I imagined a shark had popped out of the water and caught me.

A dead seagull is at my feet with its head bowed into the sand, its left wing extended outward and the right wing folded inward. The seagull looks to be in meditation, praying toward the north. It's a natural-looking part of my surroundings. The ocean is breaking on the nearby outcroppings and smaller waves wash onto shore a few feet away. The misty darkness makes the rocks, water and sand appear as images in a dream, no definite forms.
September 8, 1991

0814: Somewhere high in the mountains about seventeen miles west of Susanville, California. This morning I parked at a rest stop and slept. I'm overlooking a lake called Almunar.

A rather rough-looking character was parked nearby in an older car like mine. He looked the part of an old desperado in a Western movie, with a bushy black beard, a swarthy appearance. He looked mean and tough. The stocky man coughed several times near my car as he was out and about as if he wanted me to wake up. Perhaps he is a priest or minister, but I think not! I'm sure he is the same man I passed on the highway during the night before I arrived here to sleep. The hood of his car was up and he had his lights flashing and waved for me to stop. I sensed something not right, and felt it was a set-up on the deserted road high in the mountains, so I drove on without stopping. Now I drove on again toward Susanville.

This town is located on Highway 36 in northwest California, about eighty miles northwest of Reno, Nevada. The altitude there is 4,200 feet above sea level and the view looking west and north is of mountains covered with pine trees. It's a rather dry country and a gentleman at an adjoining table where I was having breakfast said they have been experiencing a drought for the past six years. The same story of a drought was told by people in eastern Oregon, Goldendale, Washington, and Arizona, as I traveled throughout the Western states.

Back on the road on Highway 395 near Doyle, California, a man with a pack train came into view on the east side of the highway. His dog was sitting on top of the last mule in the pack train looking relaxed and unconcerned. As they followed a trail beside the highway and approached a place called Laver Crossing, it was a scene from the out of the last century. I pulled over and began photographing the unusual procession.

"Hi, nice day," I said.

"Oh, fine day," replied the spirited nomad, as he rode by.

"Do you live around here?"

"This is my home," he said, pointing to his pack horses and mule with the dog on top.

"I'm a writer and bush pilot," I said as I snapped more pictures.

"Oh, you must be from Alaska," he replied.

"No, Northwest Territories. So long," I said as he continued on his way.

The sweet smell of sagebrush that I love was in the air. The air was clear and fresh as we (my Buick and I) continued south down 395 to Reno. I thought about staying in town until the following weekend to take in the Reno Air Show Races, but my itchy feet didn't want to stay in one place that long. The following morning I drove on to Lake Havasu, Arizona.

That afternoon a huge body of water came into view, with mountains in the southern background that appeared to be over 10,000 feet high. I was back in California. I thought I must have taken a wrong turn at Hawthorne, but I discovered a wonderful natural world on a large lake in the high Sierras that otherwise would have remained undiscovered by me. Once again, destiny played its role in this journey called life.

Before entering the town called Lee Vining, I took three pictures of Mono Lake, the mountain in the background which I believe is Mt. Morgan,

13,748 above sea level and other surrounding peaks. Later I saw a sign on the right of the highway reading "Lee Vining, Pop. 315, Elev. 6,780'." Leroy Vining was the first prospector to strike it rich from the mother lode east of the Sierras.

At the information center I met some hikers who had just completed the John Muir Trail hike of over 200 miles in 28 days. "We just took our time," said one of the male hikers, who was probably in his thirties and lived in the San Francisco Bay area.

I left Lee Vining and a short time later parked at a sign which gave the following information.

Owens Valley: Extending from Bishop south for 100 miles, the valley was inhabited by Indians for many years. Joseph Walker, in 1833, was the first white man to discover the valley. In 1843, John C. Fremont named the valley, a river and a lake after Richard Owens, an Army captain in his expedition to the area.

Darkness was descending over the Owens Valley and the mountains on the east side were colored orange by the fading light as I continued on 395 past Bishop to Kramer Junction.

The following morning I pulled into a rest area, somewhere in the desert west of Needles and east of Barstow. The bed in the Buick was quite comfortable and I slept soundly. I entered I-40 east on course to Needles. A new day on the open road began as I drove into a bright sun across a barren desert at 67 miles per hour on past Needles to Bullhead City, Arizona. This is just across the Colorado River from the many casinos that line the northwest bank of Laughlin, Nevada.

By noon, the temperature was 100 degrees in Bullhead City. I can't tolerate heat well, so I decided to head north for a month or so and return when the weather in Arizona cooled a bit.

I drove north through Las Vegas on 95, turned west about 60 miles north of Bently on State Highway 266, and continued until reaching the junction with Highway 168. Here I turned left and drove to Big Pines, located on 395.

A young man at a service station along 95 told me about a great shortcut to take rather than going north to Tonapah and then west to Mono Lake. This was one of the worst and most treacherous cutoffs I've ever had the misfortune to take! I went up and down three mountain passes from 7,000 to over 8,000 feet in a short distance. Going down the steep mountain side there were the huge dips in the road. As I would go into a dip and crest the top, with headlights shining toward the stars, the road would take a ninety-degree turn to the left. By the time the lights were on the road so I could see, it was almost too late to turn, and a steep ride down an almost vertical mountain waited. I had some choice words for the young man back on 95 who told me about this "time-saving, good and fairly straight" road. I missed the turnoff to Highway 168 and had to backtrack, and I began to wonder if I would live to reach Big Pine on Route 395. I nearly hit a cow that crossed the road at a snail's pace. It was open range and cattle had the right of way.

I drove high in the Sierras and turned off a gravel side road, where I fell into an exhausted sleep. The next morning I drove north to Mono Lake. The wild night drive over those passes became but a bad memory.

That morning I jotted down information from a sign close to the Mono Lake.

> *MONO LAKE: A Living Lake. Tiny growing plants called algae capture the sun's energy, then become food for brine flies and shrimp, which in turn are eaten by birds. Bottom dwelling bacteria decompose plants and enrich into detritus that fertilizes the algae, and the simple, but fragile, cycle begins again.*

Tufa towers look like calcium deposits and rise out of the lake and out of the shore where the lake used to be; they are like nothing I've ever seen on this planet. From another sign I took more information.

> *HOW TUFA TOWERS ARE FORMED: Salty Lake Water (Carbonates) + Fresh Water Springs (Calcium) = Tufa (Calcium Carbonate). Tufa forms underwater where fresh water calcium-bearing springs come up through the bottom of Mono Lake. Calcium chemically combines with Carbonate rich lake water to form calcium carbonate or Tufa. This solid material settles out, forming towers with the spring water pushing up inside them. The towers cease to grow as they are exposed to the air by the dropping lake level.*

I thought it felt like volcanic rock. More information from the sign at the lake:

BRINE SHRIMP: "A white feathery sort of worm, one-half an inch long, which looks like a bit of white thread frayed out at the side. If you dip up a gallon of water, you will get about fifteen thousand of them." Mark Twain, 1872.

Some 95 percent of the breeding California gulls in this state, about 40,000, return to Mono Lake each year. Safie Island rookeries and tremendous brine shrimp food supplies have made this a vital breeding ground. There are 800,000 eared grebes that nest here and 110 different species of migrating birds come here. Mono Lake is three times as saline as salt water. The water tasted salty and rancid. It was very clear and warm and at this high altitude I would expect a cold lake with sweet water.

Before the white man, nomadic hunters and traders dwelt along the shores. They were known as the Kuzedika Paiute, the fly-pupae eaters, for they gathered the pupae and larvae of Mono's brine flies at the end of each season.

Mono means "fly people" and "brine fly," in the language of their neighbors, the Yukut. The Yukut, who dwelt in the Yosemite region, considered the fly a delicacy.

Driving on, I entered Yosemite Park and after a steep climb I crossed Tioga Pass at 9,945 feet at East Yosemite Park. The park reminded me of Glacier National Park, except that it was much dryer. After driving through the park I headed north on I-5 and slept near Mt. Shasta.

Thursday morning, September 12th, I was sitting cross-legged at a rest stop near the Weed, California airport, after waking from a good night's sleep in my car. Facing Mount Shasta, I thought how closely it resembles Mount Fujiyama in Japan. An executive jet (a Cessna, I believe) and several Piper Cherokees faced in the direction of Mt. Shasta silently, as if in meditation. The sun was almost directly over the top of the towering giant, approximately southwest of my position. Except for a glacier on the north side that is barely visible, the mountain appeared as a blue mass outlined against the somewhat hazy sky to the south, blurred perhaps by pollution from southern California.

Driving through California just before dusk the day before, I encountered the pollution as a thick, yellow, dirty-looking mass of smelly air. I longed to drive north quickly to breathe and feel the clear air in the mountains and along the coast of Oregon. Once previously, when I had driven south along the Oregon Coast, the air was clean and fresh, but it seemed to change right at the California border and the blue skies turned yellow.

After leaving California behind and driving into Oregon on I-5, I stopped in Canyonville. The people were friendly and open in Canyonville and have a relaxed peaceful way about them and are not in a hurry. Stepping into this place is like going back a hundred years to the early West. Food is in bins, and an old scale hangs from the ceiling. My stay was pleasant and I left feeling good to be in such a place.

Back to the Oregon Coast on Highway 101, north of the Sea Lion Caves, there is a spectacular view of the vast Pacific. The Hecetta Lighthouse Station, built in 1893, is a prominent sight on the rocky coast and I stopped twice to take pictures. It was originally a kerosene-burning light that was visible for twenty miles. Now it is electric. The light keeper's house is a two and one-half story Cape Cod style.

The sun was almost touching the horizon. Turning off the coastal highway a few miles north, I came to a park-like area dedicated to the memory of a woman. There was grass and a path leading to the ocean about 200 yards away. The roar of the ocean filled my ears and my soul as I sat 150 yards from the pounding surf while a mist rolled in along the beach and up the steep hillside. The vastness was truly awesome.

The most incredible sight was before my eyes. The loud roar of the surf as it pounded against the nearby rocks gave the beautiful sound effects of a truly wild and natural setting. The rugged rock formation stretched out into the huge rushing waves and wispy clouds of pink, orange and silver colors extended across the western horizon. Huge white weathered logs had been flung far up on the beach, above the rocks a few feet below me. A speck on the vast ocean about a mile off shore was a fishing boat, riding the huge rolling waves as it slowly headed north. A sliver of moon shone bright auburn, the amber color of the western horizon, as the day slipped away and darkness descended over the Pacific.

Continuing up 101, I crossed over to I-5 south of Portland, and turned east onto I-84 toward The Dalles. It had rained during the night and the clouds were low over the mighty Columbia River, and covered the mountain tops. I was pretty scruffy, as I hadn't had a bath or shower for about four days and had only obtained a motel on two occasions on the journey to Arizona.

Friday, September 13, 1991

0940: *Asked a man in Roseburg, Oregon yesterday where I could get a good cup of coffee and he said, "I don't have any money!" He thought I was broke. I must have looked the part and now know what it's like to be looked down on as a homeless person, a down-and-outer, a bum.*

0952: *Passed a turn to Hood River and cruising at 67 MPH.*

1123: *I'm crossing the bridge at The Dalles to take the scenic drive to Goldendale. Watching wind surfers. The wind is rocking the car and creating strong large whitecaps on the Columbia River.*

A marker says: CELILO FALLS was buried deep beneath the water of the Dalles Dam, in 1957. I saw the falls here in 1953 with my buddy, Jim. The Indians used to net and spear fish at Celilo Falls.

After traveling several Western states promoting *Flight of the Red Beaver* and looking for a possible location to open a bookstore, I wrote the following in my journal:

Tuesday, October 15, 1991: *Pulled over behind a trucker along 395 about 0100 as I felt I couldn't safely go any further. The stars are bright in the stark clear air and as I step outside before lying down, I am blessed with two choruses of coyotes to the north and east as they sing their unique high-pitched howls. The moon is about half full and is west, just above the horizon.*

Wednesday, October 16, 1991

0642: *The sweetness of a new day before the sun peeps over the horizon is mine. There's a little lake below my cockpit bedroom where I spent the night. The early morning red glow in the eastern sky gives me new hope and resolve for my life.*

There are a few pine trees between me and the lake and a ridge beyond that etches a line in the campfire glow of the early morning sky. The new day is quiet, peaceful, a time to ponder life's journey.

In my dream world while sleeping beneath the clear sky, I dreamed that I met a sweet, attractive lady who became my wife and that I was happy. It would be nice to meet this special lady of my dreams.

Thirty minutes after beginning the day's drive, I arrived at a friendly looking place called Likely. It was 0730 as I opened the door and walked into the Likely Café.

Five men, two in cowboy boots, line the counter as they sit on stools and roll their dice. Not sure why unless they are rolling for a free breakfast. The men are all wearing blue jeans. Yes, now one is paying for all the coffee, so it must be a daily ritual. They continue with some good-natured banter about having to work for nothing today.

A couple, a man in suspenders and a green shirt and a woman, are behind the counter, and perhaps run and own the place. They are in their sixties, I would guess. One man in a cowboy hat has well-worn cowboy boots with spurs on.

The couple behind the counter, Kathryn and Lou Coppine, are the owners of the Likely Café. Lou said the café was really his wife's. The food and coffee was excellent. They have thirteen grandchildren. A three-year-old grandson is here and I gave him one of my cards and talked and showed him a picture of my son, Scott, flying a glider in Flight of the Red Beaver, which I autographed for them.

0834: Heading north. A big mule deer buck and four does are eating in a grain field at the northern edge of a small town called Alturas. Their coats are shiny brown and gray and they appear in perfect condition. I drove back, and saw three bucks, two does and a fawn and they are in the Modoc National Wildlife Refuge. I was told by some hunters the deer are getting smaller and smaller. They're shooting mostly spiked bucks as the bigger ones have been killed. One man said he would be afraid to shoot a deer because he would hit a hunter.

Canby, population 500, turning north on 139 with 79 miles to Klamath Falls, Oregon.

I arrived at Klamath Falls about noon, had coffee, and left for Crater Lake. Upper Klamath Lake reminded me of the Spokane area, with its lush forests and mountains. I wrote in my journal after arriving at the park:

1355: *Crater Lake National Park.*

The vision of the woman of my dreams last night is still plain. She was a good woman, pleasant and made me feel peaceful. Will I meet her in this life or the next one? It is good to know the lady of my dreams so well. She has a warmth and gentleness, a goodness about her.

High orange poles about twelve to fifteen feet high line the road, for snow measurement, mostly fir — evidence of a lot of moisture. The tolltaker's booth was closed so I got in free. Yea! Best things in life are free. How exciting this day is, cool, moist and feels great. Lake of Blue Waters Crater Lake. I like that, as blue is my color.

As usual, I wrote down interesting information from a sign.

"The ancient people who lived in the shadows of Mt. Mazama called themselves the `Makalak' the people of the marsh. They lived in coexistence with the earth subsisting on plants and waterfowl near shallow lakes at Klamath and Tule Basin. Archeological evidence indicates these people withstood the destruction of Mt. Mazama (Crater Lake).

To the Klammath and Modac Indians, the descendants of the Makalak, Crater Lake was a sacred place, one of great spiritual power. Some bathed in its water to seek visions and make contact with the spirits, returning home with greater wisdom and strength. (Visitor Information, William C. Steele Center, average annual snowfall 544 inches)"

It's mid-afternoon and I am sitting in a stuffed chair at the park headquarters. When I walked in I had an incredible feeling of peace and that all would be well in my life. This is a place of spiritual healing.

I can breathe again. I'm at home here in the Pacific Northwest.

Climbing up a steep road but haven't glimpsed the lake yet. I stop as a lady with a stop sign raised is standing at the front of the snow line. My journey of the past half year has led me here a place to find my way.

1342: Glimpsed the lake it is an incredible blue even though the sun is not shining through the overcast sky. I learn that about 6,800 years ago, a violent eruption transformed Mount Mazama and created a six-mile caldera that now holds Crater Lake.

This is truly one of the great events of my life, to view this magnificent lake inside this crater. A small volcano rises inside Crater Lake; a minor eruption created the smaller volcano that became Wizard Island. Centuries of snow and rain filled the caldera.

The deep blue of the lake is the most incredible blue that I've ever witnessed. A wind twister begins in front of me. The wind is raw cold and I have my heavy jacket on. The trees are 2,000 years old.

I took several pictures of Crater Lake, two with me in them taken by a gentleman from back East.

Crater Lake Lodge 1601: Looking at my baked potato covered with cheese and my hot chocolate tastes great. I was quite cold from the winter-like wind above the lake. Talked to a food handler who served me my chili and potato.

"Are there any fish in the lake? I don't suppose there are."

"Oh yes, they planted several different species but they quit planting because they did so well. You can fish for them and they have a tour boat that goes to Wizard Island but that's the only boat on the lake. You can't bring your own boat."

An interesting lady, about seventy years old, was working in the lodge and staying at the girl's dorm. She told me she got tired of staying home and watching TV, so decided to spend the summer here working and loves it. She is really about twenty-five years old inside and a delight to

Larry's grandson, Daniel, sits on the hood of the 1978 blue Buick that Larry lived in for nearly a year while he traveled the western United States and Canada promoting my first book.

visit with. I love people who take risks and experience new adventures.

We left the lodge, the Buick and I, and drove west to follow the road around Crater Lake, going in a clockwise direction.

It's 2012 as I write in front of my headlights near a ledge that overlooks Crater Lake. The eerie mist comes in waves, the wind blows strongly from the west and is quite verbal. It is a joy to be here, looking below the ledge where I saw the lake a few hours ago. Now it's a dark void covered with mist.

We drove on into the dark misty night, the blue Buick and I. We pulled off the road on a hill overlooking the Columbia River about fifteen miles south of Goldendale on the north (Washington side) of the river, about one hundred yards north of Stonehenge, where I slept in the car.

Thursday, October 17, 1991; *Am sitting on a rather comfortable rock, about 100 feet northwest of Stonehenge. I gaze westward at majestic Mt. Hood that overlooks the Columbia Gorge and the Columbia River about a mile down the hill from my eagle perch on the old volcanic rock ledge. The sky is clear and a few fair weather cumulus are near Mt. Hood, which is the farthest land I can see on the western horizon.*

A hawk is soaring by my ledge a few feet higher, working the updrafts created by the west wind blowing up the gorge.

This is a priceless view of dry, mostly grass-covered slopes with a few trees and orchards along the Columbia beneath my feet, with the snow-covered peaks rising in the west. Pondering what to do as I think of heading to Goldendale for breakfast.

A friendly encounter: "Hi, would you take a picture of me?"

"Let my husband do it."

"Just push the button on the top."

"OK."

"I'd like to buy a book, will you autograph it?" Mary asks.

"Sure."

We talk for a few minutes before this delightful and friendly couple, Lester and Mary Bushane from Palestine, Illinois, and their friends leave for the Maryhill Museum.

Stonehenge: a lasting reminder of the works of Samuel Hill, patron of this region.

Sam Hill established a townsite here with a post office, hotel, general store, nearly ten miles of roads and the Maryhill Museum three miles to the west all on his own land. His tomb is fifty yards distant, on the opposite side of the monument. This Stonehenge is a duplicate in size and original form of England's famous Stonehenge (dated 900 1350 BC) in the Salisbury Plain in Wiltshire.

When Hill, a Quaker pacifist, visited England during the 1914-1918 conflict, he saw Stonehenge and was told it had been used for human sacrifice to a pagan god. He remarked, "After all our civilization, the flower of humanity still is sacrificed to the god of war on fields of battle." From that inspiration came this monument, built by Hill. On July 4, 1918, the altar stone was completed. The full structure was completed and dedicated May 30, 1929.

Today, the sacrifice legend is generally discredited. Current belief is that Stonehenge was a device used by Stone Age astronomers to measure time and mark seasons of the year by observing positions of the sun and moon.

1121: *Sitting cross-legged on a clump of grass in front of a large granite monument about six-and-a-half-feet tall and five-feet across that sits on a concrete and rock slab.*

It's a simple yet unique tombstone that's perched on a ledge on the north side overlooking the Columbia Gorge and the Columbia River that, in Hill's days, ran free without dams. A mile or so below and a few miles west was Celilo Falls, where the Indians speared and netted salmon, which I saw as a boy.

You can see up the river east a few miles, but west is a sweeping view of the Columbia that goes many miles downstream before it disappears about the rock-terraced hillside of a slope on this side (north) of the gorge. Beyond there, past the river and rising above the gorge, is a fine view of snow-covered Mount Hood that I see even as I write these words. Three miles west is the Maryhill Museum that he built, but I don't see it. The tombstone monument reads: "Samuel Hill, 1857 1931. Amid Nature's Great Unrest He Sought Rest."

He made quite a mark, this man whose remains lie a few feet north of me. Now his physical being is gone from the world, but his memory lives on in the worthwhile things he did with his hands. The resource he accumulated stands before me as a living testament to a man with a great vision and vivid dreams that he lived and created. This man, I think, had a good heart.

Canada geese are honking down by the river as the traffic across the river on the freeway hums. The wind blows around my ears and the exposed skin of my hands, neck and face, but the warmth of the sun on my back penetrates and keeps me comfortable as I look at Samuel Hill's last resting place a few feet away.

Perhaps Samuel Hill is in a better world, a spirit world, able to soar to the heavens above, to experience the stars that are so numerous. I'm hoping that this will be my destiny-to soar to the heavens when I finish my earthly journey and continue my learning on the other side.

Samuel Hill lived his three score and ten, plus a few extra years, and he evidently had a full life.

After visiting Samuel Hill's burial place, I walked up the trail some 200 feet away to Stonehenge.

1248: Cranked up the blue Buick, on course to Goldendale. Stopped at a roadside attraction from here you can see Mount Hood fifty miles away at 11,245 feet; Mount St. Helens, seventy miles at 8,365 feet; Mount Adams, forty-five miles and 12,307 feet; and Mount Rainier, eighty-five miles and 14,410 feet.

As we drove up the northern Washington side of the scenic highway toward Goldendale, we broke over the top of the bluff that rises above the Columbia. The surrounding country is checkered by grain fields with forests starting at the north edge of town.

After the steep climb, the view was magnificent, with flat farmlands, rolling wooded hills and mountains beginning on the northern edge of the scenic town of Goldendale. Mount Rainier, Mount St. Helens, and Mount Hood are all visible. Goldendale is the county seat for Klickitat County and the sturdy courthouse speaks of an earlier age, much as the homes do. Driving through Goldendale reminded me of Spokane in the 1940s and 1950s. It was a quiet and peaceful place, a good town to live in and raise children. I liked this quiet town as I drove down Main Street past the Klickitat County Courthouse. Main Street looks as if you are stepping back in time forty or fifty years, with cars parked at an angle to the curb.

Bob, the Goldendale barber, gave me a short, good haircut, the kind I wanted, and best of all, he talked about Goldendale. He's been here many years. "There's 2,000, no about 3,000 here now. That's about double the population from the time I arrived," he said.

That afternoon, I am sitting on the asphalt taxi way at the airport a few miles north of town, looking at a Luscombe and an old cabin, weathered and sinking into the yellow grass. Mount Adams rises beyond. There are rolling grain fields to the northwest, west and south. Frost covers the mountains to the north and to the south are the open level tops of the

Columbia River gorge. The wind blows softly from the southwest, bending the grass slightly as a bird chirps nearby. This is the quietist town with cordial people that I have encountered for quite some time. I like it here. What a peaceful place at this quaint airport. A man can think and contemplate the important issues of life, like flying, writing and where to be.

A van drove up and down to the end of the taxi way. On the way back toward the road, the man asked if I needed a lift to town or some help.

"No, just enjoying the setting, took a picture of that Luscombe, with Mount Adams in the background. Third time I've been here in the last month or so."

"I've lived here since I was three. Dad and I have some old tractors at the town museum. I like this place and the quiet life in a small town."

"I'm a writer and pilot and am writing a sequel to this book, Flight of the Red Beaver. *I just got a haircut in town."*

"Oh, by Bob Walsta?"

"Yes. My name's Larry Whitesitt."

"Mine's John Halm. I'm a mechanic at the Chevy garage, also a volunteer fireman. I've got to go now, nice meeting you."

"Goodbye."

After leaving Goldendale, I drove north and then east toward Spokane.

CHAPTER 5

Grand Canyon and Bisbee

On Monday, October 21, 1991, I left Spokane and began writing in my journal:

> 0747: *Overcast clouds covering Mica Peak. Today we head south to Apache Junction, Tucson, Bisbee, Arizona, and I reckon a winter in Arizona.*

> 1226: *Leaving Liberty Lake Conoco Station. Cranked up the Buick after a fill-up, on course for Apache Junction, Bisbee and Tucson with 700 books on board.*

> 1632: *Red Lion, Missoula, Montana. Autographed a copy of Flight of the Red Beaver to Layne Spence, a waiter and student at the college (University of Montana) here. Layne's a bright young man who is studying to be a teacher. Ate a good hamburger and now it's time to go.*

After driving through Idaho, Montana, Utah and parts of Arizona, I ended up on the north rim of the Grand Canyon just before dark and wrote the following in my journal:

Friday, October 25, 1991

> *1817: Pacific time at the lodge on the north rim of the Grand Canyon.*

There's 1,200,000 acres in the Grand Canyon. The park ranger said he winters here but said, "It's not plowed for forty-five miles and we stock up on food and snowmobile for forty-five miles." Fourteen to twenty people stay here. "Seventy-five inches of snow we read a lot!" The ranger said he can hike down into the Grand Canyon and up the other side in about eight to nine hours, but his wife can jog it in about four hours. The helicopter takes eight or nine minutes. The altitude is about 8,000 feet above sea level. We sang along with the ranger "This Land Is Your Land" and "I Love To Go A-Wandering."

Cold air blows around my face and rattles the papers of my journal. My feet are on a rock wall that keeps one from dropping off the north rim into the Grand Canyon.

It's 2130 as the beautiful songs of a quartet drift through the huge double doors from inside the massive stone lodge. The cold but refreshing breeze chills my face and ears and sends a chill through my bones, in a refreshing, good kind of way.

It's fourteen miles down to the bottom of the Grand Canyon from the north rim and five to six miles from the south rim. Dale Schantz gave the slide presentation and showed a ten-minute movie of rafting down the Colorado. The north rim is much more isolated and a more pristine area of pine tree forest than you find on the south rim, which is much more commercialized and accessible.

Saturday, October 26, 1991

0630: *I'm in the high desert below the north rim of the Grand Canyon and near the Colorado River on the side of A-89 where I slept in the Buick. The day is breaking with a clear sky colored light blue, amber and yellow. Silhouetted against the eastern horizon are the rims of cliffs with jagged tops. One is shaped like a man's head, seen as if he's lying on his back. Below him is the shape of a woman's head; she is also lying on her back, her breasts pointing skyward and a bulge in her tummy indicating that she's pregnant. They are resting, waiting for the sun to awaken them.*

On my left, north of where I'm sitting, is an incredible series of red rock cliffs, extending northeast as far as I can see, with a red-tinged layer of stratus clouds overhead. I'm going to try and get a photo. Hopefully the light will be sufficient.

The road is empty as far as I can see in both directions, so much space without a sign of man. I love this high desert, the feeling of aloneness, of being one with my creator. I can appreciate the Indian's awe and respect of nature, of their god, of their view of the world.

Early morning before dawn is a most special time for me. I loved to crank up the Red Beaver and be gone in the Yukon skies, the only one in the visible sky before other humans were stirring. A rabbit runs across the road from the north and a crow flies over head as we drive down the open road.

At the Champlin Fighter Museum in Mesa, I saw for the first time a Messerschmitt ME 109, the Focke-Wulf (FW) 190, a British Spitfire and the large American Thunderbolt fighter.

The Pima Air Museum just south of Tucson was a fantastic experience. President Kennedy's DC-6, President Eisenhower's Lockheed Constellation (Connie), a B-17 in mint condition, a B-29 and other World War II warplanes sent chills up my spine as I felt the presence of the past.

I touched the leather chair in which President Kennedy sat, inside the Presidential Aircraft (Air Force One) used by Presidents Kennedy and Johnson in 1961, a DC 6-A. Close by was President Eisenhower's plane, a Lockheed VC-121A Constellation transport, 1949-1972. This was the same kind of plane in which I flew to Hawaii to catch my ship, the USS Hassayampa. Thousands of airplanes built from the 1960s on were there. About a mile away, in an airplane graveyard, hundreds of huge B-52s were lined up, their usefulness over.

The stories these planes could tell, of the men who flew them and were part of the crew it's all history and silent monuments to a time past.

Later in the afternoon I headed south to Bisbee, Arizona, and Tucson slipped behind. Around dark we stopped at the Tombstone Cemetery. I read an inscription.

In Memory of Frank Bowles. Born August 5, 1828. Died August 26, 1880. As you pass by, remember that as you are so once was I, and as I am, you soon will be. Remember me.

I visited this grave for the first time in 1975, when I was in my thirties, and I remembered it well. Life seemed to stretch on almost forever then. The wings of time have quickly brought me past the half-century mark and their beat quickens with each passing day.

Driving on to Bisbee, Arizona, I stopped at the Renaissance for a bite to eat and autographed two books: one for Joe Miller, and one for Edmund Omar Craford and Ernie & Eunice White. Fellow aviators, we swapped tales about flying at that small café near the Mexican border.

Copper Queen Hotel-Saloon, November 4, 1991

The time is 2147 as I sit in a comfortable brown leather chair (looks quite old, feels good the way leather does) in the lobby of the Copper Queen Hotel in Bisbee, Arizona. A few feet left of me is the open stairway, with a wooden railing. There are two other leather chairs nearby; an old table and a leather couch is on the opposite (east) side. Another couch is on the opposite wall, next to a wooden stool with an old typewriter on it.

It's about 2200 and I should find a place to park my car and sleep soon.

The menu has a picture of the five-story hotel and says: "When the doors of Bisbee Copper Queen Hotel opened on February 22, 1902, its owner had no idea it would become the oldest continuously operating hotel in Arizona. Built on the side of a hill, the Copper Queen Hotel was established to serve the interests of the Copper Queen Consolidated Mining Company (later becoming the Phelps Dodge Corporation) during the turn of the century era. Bisbee, with a population of 20,000, was the world's largest copper mining operation and the hotel played host to businessmen and travelers, and became the town's social center.

Designed in Italian style by Van Block and Goldsmith of New York, the hotel's floor plan was considered the most efficient that any architect *could conjure. The seventy-five-room, four-story hotel took eight months to build at a cost of $175,000. The hotel's interior was richly furnished with expensive hardwoods and California redwood trim. The forty guest rooms were beautifully furnished with large brass and iron bedsteads with large box spring mattresses and exquisitely decorated with fine draperies and carpets. The kitchen was equipped with the latest appliances, including steam dishwashing machines. Only through respect for the past can we prepare for the future.*

The hotel was the gathering place for politicians, mining officials and travelers, and patronized by men like General "Black Jack" Pershing and young Teddy Roosevelt. Brewery Gulch, site of the Muheims's Brewery, stretched around the corner with forty bars to entertain the raucous mining crowd."

I think to myself that Young Teddy Roosevelt and General "Black Jack" Pershing walked through this lobby and no doubt sat in this room, perhaps where I'm sitting. How fascinating, and to think that this day I walked the passageway of Air Force One, into President Kennedy's private bathroom. I touched his leather chair, one built for his injured back, and walked through the Press Corps and Secret Service sections, the extra pilot and copilot section. I looked into the cockpit of the DC-6 that was Air Force One along with the Boeing 707; the DC-6 was used for airports that weren't long enough for the 707. The DC-6 could get off any airport fully loaded at any altitude or temperature in 4,000 feet. A touch of history was my privilege today. Thank you God for this day.

Am enjoying this room. It's a quiet place to write and feel the ghosts of the past in this unique setting. I sold three books today.

2227: Standing in front of a picture of Walter Swan holding his book, me n' henry, in front of his One Book Bookstore in Bisbee, Arizona.

November 5, 1991

It's 0655 as I look at my wristwatch while lying on my Buick bed, propped up on my left elbow, tucked into my warm blue down-filled sleeping bag.

The day is clear and the sun is shining on some nearby western mountain tops, but hasn't yet peeked over the mountain that shades my car. Slept fairly well, but moved a couple of boxes under my foamy to get more comfortable.

Walked the streets of Bisbee until about midnight last night. A police car passed me slowly, went around the block and checked on me again as I was the only one on that street. I guess I'm a suspicious-looking character. Who would be window shopping at that hour, I suppose he was thinking. But it was so fascinating and I found the One Book Bookstore that was my main reason for coming here.

It's 0708 and the sun has popped over the eastern mountain and is shining through my rear window to brighten up my inside bedroom-cockpit world. Time to get dressed and drive into Bisbee. I keep thinking of a song that says Bisbee, Arizona. Feel good and really liked the place last night.

0732: I'm sitting parked in my movable office, writing on the blue sheet-covered foam that lays on top of my boxes of books. We're facing north, at a parking lot that says "No overnight RV parking." Across Main Street on the northwest corner is a brick-front building that says "Charles A. Tuell, DPSPC & Associates." Next to that is the Renaissance Café, where I had good coffee and homemade chocolate cookies and sold two books last night. It's small but cozy. Next, continuing eastward, is a large sign that says "LYRIC." A school bus picks up two girls and three boys standing a few feet from the car. At 1046 I'm talking to Walter Swan at his office, The One Book Bookstore. A sign says: "Always be kind. Have a good attitude. Never give up. - Walter Swan"

We exchanged books and I picked Walter's brain on operating a one-book bookstore, which is something I considered doing. He gave me some pointers on promoting and having an image people would recognize. Walter wears bib overalls and a full-brimmed farmer's hat. He's about seventy years old and his book, me 'n henry, is about his brother, Henry, and Walter growing up in Arizona in the 1920s and 1930s. It's a heartwarming story about two close brothers and it's quite humorous.

Walter is in Ripley's *Believe It Or Not* as the only person to own a one-book bookstore. He was on David Letterman's show and other TV shows. I was glad to meet Walter and enjoyed reading his book. He has been successful with his store and the trip to see Walter at Bisbee was most helpful. I learned that he has his store name patented so no one else can use it.

I drove north on I-10 back to the Pima Air Museum in Tucson. While in Arizona I visited Wickenburg, Prescott, (the old capitol of the Arizona Territory), Quartzite, Parker, and Lake Havasu.

While traveling around the state, I talked to different store owners who depended on the tourist trade to sell their arts and crafts and souvenirs. They said that since the Gulf War, the number of tourists visiting Arizona was down substantially and the tourists were spending very little money.

Book sales for me were slow, so I decided to return to the Northwest and ended up in northern Idaho near a favorite place of mine, beautiful Lake Coeur d'Alene.

Shortly before Thanksgiving, I began autographing books at the Book Warehouse in nearby Post Falls, Idaho, which is about seven miles west of Lake Coeur d'Alene. Angie Bissell, the assistant manager, helped me set up and worked out the details. Over the Thanksgiving and Christmas holidays, I autographed and sold about 500 books. Angie lives a few miles south of Harrison by Shingle Bay and lets me know when she spots loons on the lake.

On the morning of December 26, 1991, when I arrived at the book store to begin autographing for the day, I received a message to call my sister and learned that my mother had died. Mom, a tall attractive woman and heavy smoker had been battling lung cancer. Losing both parents in less than two years left a deep void and emptiness.

Family was their life and I remember with fondness those special family dinners and get-togethers at their home on East 32nd in the Spokane Valley. Good memories are mine of this special, loving couple who were my parents and good friends. They both worked very hard and provided us four children with an excellent home.

On Tuesday, December 31, while autographing books at the Book Warehouse, a man from Edmonton, Alberta, paid me one of the nicest

Angie Bissell and Larry at the Book Warehouse, where he signed and sold 500 copies of his first book at Christmas 1991.

compliments about *Flight of the Red Beaver* when he said, "I enjoyed reading your book. It's a book for the common man."

New Year's Day, 1992, I watched a magnificent bald eagle land on the top of a tree by Beauty Bay overlooking beautiful Lake Coeur d'Alene.

In mid-January I returned to Jackson Hole, Wyoming, with a carload of books to get a feel for that country in the wintertime and perhaps open a one-book bookstore of my own. I first visited Yellowstone National Park in September, 1991, and was awed by the Grand Teton Mountains near Jackson Hole. The Tetons are part of my favorite Rocky Mountains. The residents of Wyoming were down-to-earth people. They reminded me of the people I knew in Montana when I was on Desert Lookout near Glacier National Park in 1959.

I decided to return to Idaho for the winter and perhaps come back to Jackson Hole another time.

Later in the winter of 1992, I spent some time at Sandpoint, Idaho. I rented a space in the enclosed Cedar Creek Bridge in downtown, now home to retail stores for the big catalogue company Coldwater Creek, and autographed *Flight of the Red Beaver*. The bridge was a tourist attraction and there were several arts and craft stores inside.

In the spring of 1992, I spent two weeks with Scott and Stacy and helped them to sell their home in Ballard.

During the thirteen days I held their open house, about 200 people came through, usually around 1030 until about 1815. The open house signs were out in front of the house and on two busy nearby streets.

One day Scott and I felt the need to leave and do some serious hooky playing. We both wanted to relax and recharge our batteries, so we jumped into Scott's red pickup and headed north to LaConner and Deception Pass in northern Washington State. The tulips and other flowers, thousands of acres it seemed, were in bloom as we neared LaConner.

Driving into the town of LaConner, we parked on a hill on the east side of town by some turn-of-the-century two-story Victorian houses. Walking down the hill, we did some window shopping and decided to get some good fish and chips at a tavern on a saltwater channel that connects to Puget Sound. The fresh salt air, the sunny day and the quaint town all led to a unique adventure for me as this was my first time here; Scott had been here before. The fish was great and the coffee had a good bite. We walked to a nearby motor inn and looked at the great woodwork in the lobby and one of the rooms.

From there we drove to Deception Pass. It's a narrow channel that comes in from the ocean between two narrow, almost vertical rock cliffs. The current is very strong and the high bridge spanning the two cliffs is several hundred feet above the churning water. We parked the car and walked across the bridge. Looking over the bridge railing gave me a dizzy feeling and I gripped the railing.

After walking across the bridge to the south side, we descended a steep trail to the sea below and beach-combed. Skipping rocks along the swiftly moving waters, exploring some huge boulders, sitting on a white weathered old log high on the bank, we enjoyed the fresh breezy salt air, the freedom of the day and the special time together. As we drove back to Ballard, we felt it was a day well spent.

The effort we put into holding the open houses was also time well spent. After I returned to Spokane, we sold Scott and Stacy's home to a Mr. and Mrs. Hill who looked at it during that period.

On Monday morning, March 16, Scott helped me load the Buick and I departed for Spokane. The day was overcast and I felt good driving back to the hometown where my journey in life began over a half-century ago. Some black paint marks on my white jeans would remind me of the black squares

I painted on Scott's basement floor. Soon Scott and Stacy would move to the Spokane area. They were thinking of building on some acreage north of Rathdrum close to Twin Lakes that Scott's grandparents, the Parks, had left for their children and grandchildren.

When I was at Scott's I made the decision to go ahead and write the sequel to *Flight of the Red Beaver*. During the early part of my stay there, I mentioned to Scott that I might just add a few chapters to *Flight of The Red Beaver* because of the draining, time-consuming effort and cost. But one day while staying there I decided to go for it. I knew I wouldn't be satisfied or feel complete without doing the full sequel. So, the die was cast!

On my trip home I stopped at Ellensburg for a hamburger and several cups of coffee. It was raining over Snoqualmie Pass and I encountered a downpour around Cle Elum, but it was dry in Ellensburg and the sun was trying to show itself.

On Saturday, March 21 Scott called and together via long distance, we wrote up the earnest money purchase agreement for the purchase of his home, faxed it back and forth until it was perfect, and closed the sale. It all went smoothly because we worked so well together.

The following Wednesday, I was sitting on a point of land near a lighthouse at Tubbs Hill. The waters splashed against the rock peninsula as I sketched the quiet little bay, a boat, the mountain, six seagulls flying east — recording the beautiful world of Lake Coeur d'Alene. Seagulls gave their piercing cry and the waters surrounding me gave a quiet calm voice to my soul.

Mom and dad went to Tubbs Hill on their first date.

Thursday, March 26, 1992

1515: *Lying on the grass at Liberty Lake Park, listening to ducks, red-winged blackbirds, the ribit ribit of the frogs, a woodpecker's bill and various other creatures of the marsh and forest. High overcast, and the sun is barely burning a hole through as I hike above Stone Bridge.*

2315: *Lying in my nice bed, thinking of my flight north this summer, if it works out, and the name of my book.*

It was one year and two days ago when the blue Buick and I drove down

I-90 toward Seattle with 500 books and began an incredible adventure to promote and sell *Flight of the Red Beaver*. This journey covered over 50,000 miles in the Western United States, especially the Pacific Northwest area, and into British Columbia, Canada.

Many events during this journey had a profound effect on my life, teaching me anew the basic important things in life's journey: how to live each precious new day and to appreciate the beauty of God's perfect creation. I came to the stark realization of the short time allotted humans and began to understand the important issues of life. In many ways it was a hard year, but it was packed full of adventure. For one year I derived my livelihood from the sale of my book *Flight of the Red Beaver*.

CHAPTER 6

Flying North into the Past

"Hi Scott. How you doing?"

"Hi, Dad, just wanted to see you before you left and see you off!"

It was Saturday morning, May 23, 1992, as I walked into the Skyway Café on the south side of Felts Field, inside the terminal building. Scott was eating breakfast and I joined him at his table near the window, where we had a good view of airplanes taxiing by to the active runways 21 Right and 21 Left. We could see the planes landing and taking off. We talked about the important issues of life airplanes and flying.

"Dad, would you take me for a flight before you leave?"

"Sure, Scott, I'll take you up before I leave for Canada."

"Let's go and get the plane ready."

"I've also got to file a flight plan to Penticton, British Columbia where I'll be clearing customs."

It was good to see my son this morning, an unexpected but welcome visit. After the sale and closing of their home in Ballard, Scott and Stacy moved to the Spokane Valley and rented an apartment until they could build their dream home in northern Idaho along a creek just south of Twin Lakes. We live about four miles apart and it's great to be so close!

After filing a flight plan in the Flight Service Station above the Skyway Café with a proposed departure of 1230, Scott and I drove to Felts Field Aviation and checked with the woman at the desk about the Cessna 172 I had booked for two weeks.

"The airplane is ready to go. We changed the oil and put in several extra quarts of oil for your trip," she replied.

"Thanks, I'm going to take my son for a short flight before I head north."

The familiar loading of the plane began, just like the days when Scott and I would load the Red Beaver for a flight into the northern wilderness: the sleeping bag, fishing tackle, and other light things in the rear and the food and heavier items toward the front of the plane, right behind the two front seats.

After loading the plane and locking up my car, I dropped my car keys at the office and we walked back to the airplane that I flew alone to the Arctic in 1989. The ship, a Cessna 172, 734 UW, and I flew to Tuktoyaktuk, an Inuit (Eskimo) village near the mouth of the mighty McKenzie River along the shores of the Arctic Ocean in the Northwest Territories, and then south to Inuvic and west to the farthest northern settlement in the Yukon, Old Crow. We were well acquainted and I trusted this ship with my life, after safely flying thousands of miles over some of the most rugged and remote wilderness areas in the world. She's a good ship, very reliable, and we know each other well.

After a good pre-flight walk around, checking the wing tanks to make sure they were topped, the oil, and the general safety conditions of the airplane, we climbed aboard. After calling out the open window, "Clear" and making sure no one was in the vicinity of the prop, I cranked her up, called Felts Ground Control, reported my position, requested permission to taxi, and was told to taxi and hold short of Runway 21R. We taxied toward the active runway and did our run-up just south of the runway, off the taxi way at a designated area.

After a satisfactory run-up, we were cleared to depart Runway 21R. After taxiing to the middle of the runway and applying full throttle, we began to roll, slowly at first, but soon we were at 55 knots, and with slight back pressure on the elevator control, we lifted off and experienced once again the freedom and magic of flight that Scott and I know so well. It was good to have my copilot from the old days in the Yukon with me once again.

We made a right-hand climbing turn and at 1,000 feet turned right again, flying east over Beacon Hill, north of the field, on our downward leg. We were cleared to land on Runway 21R and, as with the day before, there was a strong breeze from the southwest. We received a lot of lift off Beacon Hill and descended rather slowly on the base and final leg, because of the lift; we landed well past the numbers, in fact, a fair ways down the runway. It didn't really matter because Felts Field Aviation is at the far west end of the field, but as a pilot you normally try to set your ship down close to the beginning of the runway by the numbers. A few days before this flight when I was doing my biannual check ride with the flight instructor, the wind was much stronger from the same direction and again two landings were long at Felts. However, at the Deer Park Airport, where we did some touch and go landings, we made some respectable short field landings.

A few weeks previously I had a flight physical by Dr. Baird, an avid, cheerful pilot who flies out of Felts Field. On the eye chart, my vision was 20/15 each eye; however, closeup vision is showing the aging process, as I wear reading glasses.

After we touched down, we taxied to Felts Field Aviation, where Scott got out.

"I love you, son."

"I love you, Dad."

I taxied again toward the active runway and held short of 21R. After getting clearance from the tower to taxi onto the active runway and depart, we accelerated more rapidly without the 200+ pounds of my son and quickly left the runway at 1230 and opened our flight plan with Felts Flight Service Station. The estimated time of arrival was at 1400, for 1 hour and 30 minutes of flight time. We made a right-hand departure and headed north for several miles to get clear of traffic and then turned northwest to our heading of 305°, flying direct to Penticton, British Columbia.

A little east of the Mead Airport, as I was climbing and at about 6,000 feet, three white blossoms opened off my port wing to the west. They were skydivers dropping to the Mead Airport far below. You can usually see divers jumping here on weekends during good weather.

The engine roared smoothly, reassuringly, as I scanned the familiar lakes, valleys, and mountains in the area where I grew up. Loon Lake lay only a few miles north of my course and a few miles farther away was Deer Lake, where I would go to a church camp as a kid, catch a bunch of frogs, swim, and eat candy for a week in the summer.

The Spokane River was a few miles south off the port wing. At 1229, we were approaching Lake Roosevelt at 8,000 feet above sea level. This large lake, created behind Grand Coulee Dam, was a familiar sight from this perspective. I was on the same course, in the same airplane, as I had been on September 1, 1989, when I headed north to Penticton, British Columbia to clear customs.

My ship and I were one as we flew through the smooth air, on a clear, sunny day with visibility unlimited.

At 1305 we were over Inchelium. This Indian village had more meaning and a personality of its own for me since I flew over here in 1989. About ten miles west of Inchelium are North and South Twin Lakes, which to me are like a touch with the past, as they remind me of so many northern lakes on which I've landed a float plane in Canada.

One day a good woman friend of mine (who also loves the loon) and I spent the good part of a day at North Twin Lakes watching a nesting pair of the common loon. Their nest was located at the north end of the lake in a somewhat marshy area on a spit of land that was about two feet above the water level. The cry of these loons was like lonely haunting voices of my far northern past, as their voices carried across the lake to where we were watching with binoculars, and sent chills up our spines.

These elusive magnificent black and white birds have piercing red eyes, a dark green head, bodies that are three feet in length, and a wingspan of five feet which gives them a majestic appearance on the lake as they glide over the surface or dive to a depth of 200 feet catching fish. Once I saw a loon swimming underwater close to the seaplane dock at Watson Lake. It was chasing a fish and was just a blur of black and white, streamlined similar to a long bullet. The male and female look identical. Each year a pair of loons will lay one or two eggs. The young chicks often ride on the backs of their parents for protection from large fish below or silent eagles soaring overhead. Usually only one pair of loons nest on a lake, as they are a solitary bird and very territorial. Their lifespan can be 20 years or more.

When I had my place on the shores of Watson Lake in the Yukon, the loons were usually one of the first birds to arrive in the spring. Their voices in the morning before I began my first flight and in the evening when I finished my last flight were truly the call of the wilderness that sent chills through my being.

My friend and I spent many hours watching this pair. They would take turns sitting on the nest. As one swam toward the nest the other loon would get off the nest, swim out and greet its partner with a loon nuzzle, and then begin its fishing: gliding along the water, putting its head beneath the surface looking for fish and then diving, sometimes for quite a distance.

My friend and I once drove to Hatheume Lake in southern British

Columbia and watched some of the loons there. The rough, somewhat gravel-rutted road that we took off the highway was about fifteen miles long. On that particular lake there is a relatively large loon population (about ten or twelve).

A fishing lodge with log cabins sits on the northeast side of the lake. You can only catch and release fish at this lake; however, there are lakes close by where you can keep your catch. There were three loons about fifty feet from the boat dock, waiting for some fishermen to begin catching and releasing the fish. The loons, being a very intelligent bird, discovered that when a fish was caught and released, it was a bit stunned and easy to catch. It's a great pleasure to get close to a loon for pictures as they will swim to within a few feet of the boat.

As we continued to watch the loons, we received five additional special gifts that day at North Twin Lakes. A cow moose with two offspring, almost fully grown, came wading through the marsh, about 150 yards behind the loon nest. They were in a playful carefree mood, enjoying the water and the tender plants they ate off the marsh floor, often dipping their heads into the water to pull up a succulent plant. Two other moose strolled through the marsh that afternoon. We watched them with the naked eye and then with our binoculars.

That was a very special day that I often remember and relive.

If I were to come back as one of God's creatures and had a choice, I would like to be a loon, flying north every year to a wilderness lake (I love to fly), where I would spend the summer with my mate, make love and have a child or two most summers, then as winter approached fly south and winter along the warm California coast and swap flying stories and wilderness adventures with my contemporaries. When a "whisky front" came into Watson Lake, bush pilots told tales over large, flaming Poose Capays, a strong northern drink of seven liqueurs which warmed the insides and helped the stories to flow as we sat in the Watson Lake Hotel.

I'd love to raise my voice, sing beautiful loon songs and bring pleasure to the two-legged creatures called humans; to make them stop and appreciate the wilderness experience and then to share it with their children and grandchildren. To me, the loon is wilderness speaking!

At 1312, the air was smooth with scattered fair weather cumulus and a cloud base at 9,000 feet. Our course took us just south of Republic, Washington, and I could see the Ferry County Airport about ten miles north of there. We flew near Mt. Bonaparte, 7,257 feet above sea level, and then just north of Scott Airfield, which is a few miles south of the Canadian border and a port of entry for clearing customs in the United States.

About 1350, I changed radio frequencies and pressed the black mike button.

"Penticton Radio, this is Cessna 734 Uniform Whiskey 15 miles south, estimating the airport in ten minutes."

"Cessna 734 Uniform Whiskey, we check you 15 miles south, contact the tower on 118.5."

"Penticton Tower, this is Cessna 734 Uniform Whiskey, 15 miles south. Estimate the airport in ten minutes."

"Cessna 734 Uniform Whiskey, you are cleared for a straight-in approach on Runway 34. Be advised of an airplane making touch and go landings."

"Roger, 734 Uniform Whiskey cleared for a straight-in approach on runway 34 and I have the airplane in sight."

We made a long straight-in approach and my ship made a smooth landing a few feet beyond the numbers at exactly 1400, which was our ETA (Estimated Time of Arrival).

"734 Uniform Whiskey, you're cleared to turn left at the first taxi way."

"Thank you. Close my flight plan, please."

"Your flight plan is closed."

"Thanks."

The people operating the tower in Penticton have always been very courteous and helpful.

We taxied and parked by the tower, in front of the Spenser Aviation Shell gas pumps. I sat in the plane until a young woman customs officer came to the plane and then I stepped out. They get a bit uptight if you leave the plane before they arrive.

"Hi, how are you?"

"Oh, fine."

"Say, you're right on schedule. Are you carrying any guns or items that you plan on selling or leaving in Canada?"

"No, I'm not."

"OK, enjoy your trip into Canada."

"Say, could you give me some information on places where I might clear customs north of Skagway, Alaska, as I may fly to Skagway and then back into Canada?"

"Follow me to the office and we'll look up the nearest Canadian Customs in the area."

We walked to a small building a few hundred feet north and she gave me a list of places where I could clear Canadian customs north of Skagway.

"Thanks for your help Goodbye."

"Goodbye."

There was no one at Spencer Aviation, so I walked into the main terminal building and down a hall to the Air Radio Flight Service Station to ask where the gas man was.

"Oh, I don't know, but I'll call around and see if we can find him."

"Thanks, I'll file a new flight plan to Smithers, B.C. with a fuel stop at Williams Lake."

"OK."

I filled out the flight plan and the air radio man looked it over and added a few things.

Ten minutes later a young Indian man arrived at Spencer Aviation.

"Hi, I'm Larry Whitesitt, what's your name?"

"My name is Don Jones," and we shook hands.

"Would you top the tanks?"

"Sure."

"Do you take Visa?"

"Yes."

We had a nice visit. Everyone always seems so friendly at Penticton Airport and it's one of my favorite stops. Don Jones used my camera and took a picture of me standing next to my ship. I also took a couple of pictures of him.

After topping the tanks and checking the oil, I cranked up my ship and after contacting ground control, we were cleared to taxi to Runway 34 and then, turning to the tower frequency, we were given clearance to take off. It was about 1520 as we lifted off the Penticton Airport and began our new heading of 315° that would take us over Kamloops, and then a slight course change to 302° to Williams Lake.

The day was sunny and the air clear as we climbed over Okanogan Lake on our new heading, and I snapped a picture of the lake. As we flew over Peachland, the lake made a jog to the right (east) and we left this long, beautiful body of water.

A few miles northeast is the city of Kelowna. This is where I went to train for my Canadian commercial pilot's license and instructor's rating, which I obtained in 1967. It was shortly after getting my license that I went to work for Ominica Air Service as a bush pilot, flying a Super Cub, Cessna 185 and the wonderful Beaver.

Mt. Gottfriedsen at 6,224 feet was off my port wing a few minutes after we passed over Peachland and up ahead off the Starboard wing was Whiterocks Mountain at 6,134 feet.

A few minutes later, off our port wing, lay Douglas Lake, where there is a huge cattle ranch by that name. We passed the lake at 1550.

My original plan was to fly to the Arctic Ocean coastline at the northern tip of the Yukon Territory, northwest of Old Crow, the farthest north settlement in the Yukon. However, I wasn't sure how far I would actually go. One of the main purposes of the trip was to bring a professional photographer along to get some excellent slides of glaciers and some videos of the Kluane Park area and footage of the Arctic. Yesterday I had lunch with the photographer and when he left at 1400 he said he was going to the bank to withdraw funds for his share of the flight, as he wanted to work up a series of photos of the far north that he could sell. It was something he had dreamed of doing for a long time. He used to live in Alaska and said he had done a fair amount of aerial photography there.

When I talked to the photographer later Friday, around 1630, he informed me he wasn't going to go. I made many calls to locate a photographer, but as we were booked to take off in about 20 hours for a two-week trip, I wasn't able to locate anyone who could go on such short notice. Needless to say I was upset, but decided to fly north anyway, following my gut and my heart, as the airplane was mine for two weeks. The camera I owned had no telephoto or wide angle lens, but it did take sharp photos. Although I was initially upset when the photographer backed out, I felt there was a reason that he didn't go and that this seemingly negative happening would really turn into a positive thing for my life, and I felt it was for the best.

As my ship and I continued north farther into British Columbia, my thoughts were, "I wish Scott was with me." Why take this flight alone when you're not going to get the photos you wanted, and that was one of the main reasons for the trip?

The farther north we went, the more I thought of Scott, who was now living in the Spokane Valley, close to where I lived. Flying alone to the Arctic in 1989 was enjoyable, but now as I looked at the empty copilot seat, I really wished Scott was along to enjoy this vast country that was a big part of his life when he was a young boy and through his early teens. Scott has such a warm, good heart and it was such a joy and privilege watching him as he grew into manhood. His mother Kathy once said, "Scott is like David in the Bible," referring I guess to his good heart.

The Thompson River came into view a few minutes after passing Douglas Lake and around 1610 we flew over the town of Kamloops, located on the banks of this scenic river. We changed course to our new heading of 302° and Kamloops passed beneath us, looking very tiny at 8,000 feet, and quietly disappeared behind us.

My ship and I were flying over a vast northern land of lakes, rivers, mountains, home to the grizzly bears, wolves, mountain caribou, sheep, deer, moose and many smaller creatures of the forest. It's refreshing to have this vast space before me without any sight of other airplanes and disappearing signs of man.

We flew north for a time until my gut and heart told me it was time to make a 180° turn and return to the land of my birth. I contacted Kamloops radio and changed my flight plan back to Penticton.

Later in the day I landed at Penticton and filed a flight plan to Scott Airfield a few miles south of the U.S. Border near Oroville, Washington. Anytime you fly into Canada, you must file a flight plan — it's the law and if you don't obey it you're in deep trouble. In the United States you're not required to file a flight plan, but it's a good idea. The Canadian gentleman at the FSS (Flight Service Station) at Penticton told me how to file the flight plan and close it.

"Once you see Scott Field, contact me by radio and I'll contact Seattle Center and close the flight plan; that will get you off the hook."

"Ok, thanks for your help."

Shortly after 1800, we lifted off the runway and about five minutes later I contacted Penticton Radio.

"Penticton Radio, this is Cessna 734 UW, I have Scott Field in sight. Please close my flight plan."

"Cessna 734 UW, Roger, your flight plan is closed."

"Thank you and thanks for your help."

Scott Field is a small airport with a narrow paved runway that runs north and south. It doesn't have a control tower. Descending and flying west of the airport, the windsock told me the wind was from the north. We flew downwind heading south, made our base leg to the east and turned final into the wind on the north runway. We were getting familiar with each other again, my ship and I, and at 1820, we touched down smoothly close to the numbers.

As we taxied to the small building where the custom officer waited, I noticed several small planes in T hangars. The custom officer said I had to purchase a $25 decal to put on the plane by the door, which I did.

Looking at my sectional chart, I decided we would fly on a southeasterly course, and perhaps spend the night at Priest River, Idaho, where there is a paved strip.

We lifted off the north runway at 1840, circled once to gain altitude and flew close to Mt. Bonaparte, which is about 20 miles southeast. We flew over the Sanpoil River, crossed Lake Roosevelt, and passed over the outskirts of Chewelah, then along the mountain sides to get a little free lift. My craft and I were one and we were free of the earth's bondage for a time as we soared and dove, twisted and turned in the vast freedom of the skies.

We began our descent and flew over Usk and up the Pend Oreille River towards my sister Nancy's summer place, which is located on the north bank, seven miles northwest of Newport. Nancy and her husband, Doug, found their dream on the banks of this beautiful river and will one day retire there.

Just north of Usk, there is a herd of buffalo on the Kalispel Indian Reservation. There is also a unique place called the Bear Caves, where I sometimes go to meditate and get in touch with the natural spiritual world. Inside a rather large cave, which the Indians have used for centuries, are rock seats and a podium made of stone. As you look out of the opening, which is shaped like a bear, you can see the Pend Oreille below, a lovely valley and majestic mountains beyond. You can feel that this is a sacred place in which to worship and meditate.

The area along the Pend Oreille River and north to Priest Lake, which is crystal clear and quite large, reminds me so much of Canada. It's a somewhat remote area in which I enjoy spending time.

Flying over the river, we did a fly-by close to the water, and I could see several vehicles, but no humans at Nancy's place. We did a 180° turn upstream and flew by again over the river, but still saw no one. They might have been watching deer, as night was descending and the deer would be

Larry's sister, Nancy Furlott, and her son, Andy, at their summer place on Pend Oreille River in eastern Washington state, 7 miles north of Newport. They are in front of the Cessna 185 seaplane, which Larry had rented in 1988.

coming out to feed in the nearby fields, I thought to myself.

As we continued following the river upstream, Newport, Washington, passed below our starboard wing and Priest River, Idaho, and the airport appeared a short distance ahead. An airplane was ahead of me at a lower altitude and appeared to be heading to the Priest River Airport.

Scott was in my thoughts and plans began forming for a flight with Scott and Stacy in the next few days, as this was a long holiday weekend. Maybe we could fly to the Canadian Rockies, or perhaps to Kalispel, Montana, where Scott was born, and over Glacier Park (a favorite place of mine), or perhaps even down to the Grand Teton Mountains in the Jackson Hole country in Wyoming. We had talked about flying together to the Yukon one day and I feel that would be a worthwhile and exciting trip.

As the small town of Priest River, Idaho came closer, I decided to go farther upstream, land at the Sandpoint Airport and spend the night in this picturesque town nestled beside Lake Pend Oreille. Flying from daylight into evening, the details below, trees, hills and mountains, began to blur together into a large dark form, a peaceful transition.

This is Larry's first airplane, a Piper J-3 Cub N42200, which he purchased for $900 in the fall of 1961 when he had a total of 15 hours flying experience. This picture was taken north of the Alaska range.

The air was smooth as we continued to fly over the river that led us upstream to the Sandpoint Airport, located a few miles north of town. I first landed at this airport in our Piper J-3 Cub in 1961 on my first solo cross country flight when I had about twenty hours total flying time.

Calling on the Sandpoint Unicom frequency of 122.8, I advised other traffic that might be in the area of my position and that I would be landing.

Another airplane, a few miles east, was flying north toward the airport over the west shore of the lake. The pilot called on 122.8, reporting his position and intention to land.

I was southwest of the airport and so decided to let the other aircraft land first. I didn't think he could see me in the fading light, as I flew at a higher altitude, and we were not in any particular hurry.

About fifteen miles southeast of here is where Kathy, Scott, and I spent the summer of 1961 on Faucett Lookout. We had a beautiful view of Pend Oreille Lake from our lofty perch.

A few miles from the lookout was Bayview, a small community in a bay at the southern end of Lake Pend Oreille. When I was a small boy, my fishing pal and best friend, Grandpa Rydblom, kept his old yacht, the Susan Jo, there. One day, when I was about three years old, Grandpa let me take the helm and I turned the boat in a circle. What a thrilling and fun day that was. I remember it well!

Larry's son, Scott, and his dog, Smokey, are standing next to Faucett Lookout in the summer of 1961. The lookout overlooks Lake Pend Oreille.

A few years later the government built the Farragut Naval Training Center (boot camp) just west of Bayview. My father drove a bus from Sandpoint to the base and back to town, picking up sailors who were going on liberty and then later, after many of these young men were quite inebriated, he would drive them back to boot camp.

A few miles south of my position, on the west side of Sandpoint, was the home where my parents, brother Bob, sister Nancy and I lived while Dad drove the bus to Farragut.

One summer day while walking home from the store, snarling inhuman voices made me look up in boyhood wonder, as several World War II fighters streaked overhead and disappeared from view north of town, near where I'm now flying. That was in the summer of 1944.

My ship and I hung suspended in space for a time, and I pondered this special flight that brought me back to the land of early childhood.

The swift wings of time beat faster and faster. Almost fifty years have passed since I caught pollywogs on Lake Pend Oreille and began the first grade in a red brick schoolhouse a mile south of here. Over half a lifetime, some thirty-three years, have been spent following my first love, flying airplanes, and most of the flights have been over a magnificent northern wilderness when I lived in the Yukon.

Flying over rugged mountain peaks and landing on remote pristine lakes, God's perfect creation could be seen and felt. I experienced the wilderness

Larry's grandfather and fishing partner, William ("Bill") C. Rydblom, on his fishing yacht, "The Susan Jo," on Lake Pend Oreille in 1942.

and saw perfection.

The steady drone of the engine, the feel of the controls, and the faces of the gauges tell their story; all are familiar, yet I feel strange, as though I've been suspended in time. Life has flown by and I'm all alone. What happened to those days in the summer of 1944 when I was a young boy and World War II was being fought? What happened to all those young sailors from nearby Farragut Boot Camp who came to town looking for a date? I was six years old then and my mother was twenty-six. My age is now more than double hers then. How can that be?

My life's greatest joy was the birth of my son, Scott, watching him grow up and now seeing him living his dreams. Soon there will be a new birth in our family, as Scott and Stacy excitedly await the birth of their first child. I'm happily looking forward to being a grandfather and rather suspect this will be one of life's greatest rewards and reasons for being put on the planet Earth.

Beneath white wings, a perfect day gracefully slipped away to a friendly glow in the western sky, as I dreamed of tomorrow and new adventures in other worlds beyond the distant mountains.

CHAPTER 7

Flying Over the Rockies

Beneath our wings Runway 21 Right fell away and as we made a climbing right turn north, we passed over the Spokane River. A beautiful sky world unfolded as we began this flight to the Yukon in our trusty ship, Cessna 172, N62731.

It was shortly after 3:00 p.m., Wednesday, July 28, 1993, as we left Felts Field and the city of Spokane, Washington, behind. After many delays and seemingly endless details, we were at last free of earth's bonds and the sunny skies north beckoned warmly.

Janey Youngblood, known to me as "The Loon Lady," sat beside me in the copilot's seat, busily recording our flight with a video camera.

The first time I met Janey, she was giving a presentation to the Spokane Audubon Society on loons, which are my favorite bird. I briefly spoke about the book I wrote, *Flight Of The Red Beaver*, and mentioned it would soon be in print. Janey purchased a few of my first books and we became friends. Through the book, she became fascinated with the Yukon and said she would one day like to discover it for herself.

When I asked if she would be interested in going on this flight and taking videos of the north, she happily said, "Yes."

We could scarcely believe that we were actually flying north on a new and exciting adventure. We were flying high and in great spirits.

North of Spokane, Loon and Deer lakes made their appearance within a few minutes. Janey's home is on the north shore of Loon Lake and she

Janey Youngblood and
Larry (pictured) heading
out of Spokane on the
northern flight of dreams.

began taking videos as I positioned the plane so she could get some good
pictures.

> 1540: *We're at 8200' on a heading of 305° on course to Penticton,
> British Columbia to clear customs. This is the best day of weather we
> have had since May. Janey is taking videos of Lake Roosevelt. Inchelium
> is below the nose of our ship, to the southwest a few miles.*

Inchelium is a small town located on the west side of Lake Roosevelt on
the Colville Indian Reservation. A ferry carries cars and passengers to
Inchelium from the east side of Lake Roosevelt. North and South Twin Lakes
were clearly visible a few miles west of Inchelium, and there were nesting
pairs of loons on both of these lakes.

> 1603: *At 8,350 feet over Lake Roosevelt. Scattered fair weather cumulus
> clouds above at about 9,500 feet.*

> 1619: *A little bumpy, wings rock but it's still comfortable. Curlew Lake
> is southeast a few miles.*

> 1632: *Descending, Oliver ahead.*

We landed at Penticton and closed our flight plan. The wind was 25-30
knots from the south and it bounced us around on final, but our trusty ship set
us down safely and made a respectable landing. We taxied to the Shell gas
pumps and waited for Customs to clear us into Canada.

After about five minutes, a young, nice-looking man with a Customs
uniform walked up to the plane. "How long do you plan on staying in

Canada?"

"Oh, about seven days."

"I'll put eight days on this form in case you have weather problems."

"Okay, thanks."

"Do you have anything you plan on leaving in Canada?"

"No."

"Do you have any firearms?"

"No."

"Okay, enjoy your stay."

I've found the Customs Officers in Penticton to be friendly and very helpful. They make you feel welcome.

After clearing Customs, I asked a man at the Shell office if he would top my tanks while I checked the weather at the Flight Service Station (FSS). I set the brakes with the airplane facing into the wind.

After walking into the FSS and asking for a weather report for Williams Lake and parts north, the fuel man from the Shell office started waving excitedly outside the window. I hurried outside, where our ship was bouncing and moving. The wind had shifted 180° from south to north and the fuel man was unable to hold the plane by himself.

Together, we turned the airplane north into the wind and I again set the brakes before returning to the Flight Service Station to finish the weather briefing. The weather north was quite bad.

A small home-built airplane was coming in to land as the wind shifted 180° and suddenly, because of the wind change (wind shear), the airplane stalled. But the pilot was able to recover quickly from the stall and landed safely, although somewhat shaken.

"You can probably get a room at the Sky-Tel Motel at the south end of the field. You can taxi your airplane and tie it down in front of the motel," the air radio man replied to my questions.

"That sounds good."

"I'll call and see if there's a room available for you."

"Thanks."

A room was available at a very reasonable rate, and we taxied down and tied our ship securely to the ground in front of the motel.

At 8:32 PM, we were at the Sky-Tel Motel, weathered in, tired and in need of a good sleep. The friendly owner graciously furnished us with an older Mercedes car, only asking that we replace the gas that we used, and we drove to a restaurant a few miles northeast of the motel.

We ordered T-bone steaks and filled our plates from the salad bar. It was a good meal. After dinner we drove to a service station, put some gas in the car, and returned to the motel.

2405: Sitting on the carpet, cross-legged, with my notebook journal lying on the open sliding door track, listening to the steady fall of rain. The fresh smell of rain penetrates my body in a most pleasant and satisfying way as I watch lights reflecting off the water on a nearby runway, a hundred yards to the east. It looks like a river in the dark night.

A most unusual chorus of thunder has been mine to experience. Not the usual clap of thunder, but a long, even, distant chorus of a great orchestra. A voice from within has been talking to me for some time and now once again it tells me in the form of gentle splashing rain, "It's time to make that last flight and go on to other things. Flying has been a good, rich part of your life," the voice tells me, "but there are other worlds to experience and it's now time to explore and partake of new beginnings, new horizons with unlimited depth and breadth."

Maybe it's time to hang it up, put the pilot log books away, along with the maps and pictures, for my grandchild to one day go through and know that flying was my first love. The patter of the rain is soothing.

Often, as a bush pilot, when I was tired or had a close call, at night I would be ready to say, "I quit! No more flying for me!" But the following day, I would be eager to fly the northern skies again, so I remembered how it was and thought that perhaps I would feel differently in the morning. One lesson I think I've learned in life is to never say, "I'll never do that again."

Perhaps this inner voice talking to me was telling me this was to be my last flight north to the Yukon. Time will tell and I'll listen. My first love, airplanes, entered my life over fifty winters ago and flying is a large part of my life. It's something I think about on a daily basis.

I finally fell into a deep sleep.

July 29, 1993, 0754: Terminal Building, Flight Service Station in

Penticton, British Columbia. Last night, early hours this morning a chorus of thunder and heavy rain gave quite a display to my ears.

Feel fairly well rested, and with great coffee, I feel good. Actually feel great, indeed. Sun's trying to peep through the clouds over the airport and is succeeding somewhat for brief periods. Lower fog around the nearby hills is moving.

"Sun's peeping through. Looks great, Lars." I call myself Lars at times, when I try to figure something out. Feel ready to go north once again.

0937: Back at the motel. Checked the weather. It was not good up north and looked like it wouldn't change for awhile.

Almost decided to bag it and go back to SFF (Felts Field). As I was taxiing to the runway for take off back to the United States, I decided to stop in front of the Flight Service Station and check the weather one more time. Upon doing so, I found it was improving, so we'll continue on to Williams Lake and then decide if we could go farther north.

I had filed a flight plan to Scott Field at Oliver, Washington, located a few miles south of the Canadian border, and had phoned Customs and told them we would arrive in an hour. Janey called Customs again and canceled our appointment while I filed a new flight plan, this time to Williams Lake.

We lifted off runway 16 and flew over Skaha Lake, which begins about 200 yards past the end of the runway. When we reached 400 feet, we made a climbing left turn to our new heading of 315°. If the weather cooperated, this heading would take us over Kamloops and to Williams Lake, a distance of 212 miles, or about a two-hour flight.

We flew over beautiful Okanogan Lake for about twenty miles and left it where the lake bends to the northeast, ten miles below Kelowna.

Memories of Kelowna and the beginning of my life as a commercial pilot are many. On February 28, 1967, Doug Maccoll, who worked as an instructor for Caribou Air Charter at Kelowna, gave me my first dual lesson for my Canadian commercial pilot license. Doug was formerly on the aerobatic team when he was a pilot in the Royal Canadian Air Force. He was an excellent instructor.

We flew the Luscomb HHY, a small two-place tail dragger. It can get a bit tricky at times, especially on landing if you're not on top of the stick and the rudder controls, but is really a fun airplane to fly. I flew it across British Columbia and into the United States solo much of the time to build up flying hours needed for my commercial ticket. I had sold our Aeronca Chief CF-UVX to a couple of new pilots at Smithers and was using the money for this training.

On one flight I landed at Pangborn Field in Wenatchee, Washington to pick up a former high school classmate and friend, Dennis Rae, and we flew in the Luscomb to Smithers, British Columbia. I let Dennis fly part of the way and noticed he had a good touch and feel for flying. Later Dennis, who taught school and coached wrestling at Wenatchee, obtained his private pilot's license. Dennis, his wife Connie, and I all went to Northwest Christian High School in Spokane, Washington.

On April 24, 1967, at Pit Meadows, British Columbia, Len Mellon, a check pilot for the DOT (Department of Transport) gave me the flight examination for both the Canadian commercial pilot license and the instructor's rating, which I successfully passed in the Cessna 172 RKH.

Shortly after landing my first flying job, I made my first flight with a paying passenger in a Super Cub float plane on June 5, 1967.

On October 31, 1969, I began flight training for my U.S. commercial pilot license at Galvin Flight Service at Boeing Field, Seattle, Washington. This training was with an excellent flight instructor named Jim Gill. As a veteran I was able to use the G.I. Bill, which paid for most of the U.S. flight training. On November 5, 1969, I was issued a commercial pilot license and on December 31, 1969, successfully passed the instrument rating check ride, also at Galvin Flight Service in the Piper PA-28 9684 W.

On October 10, 1970, I began my first flight lesson in the same Piper PA-28, for the airline transport pilot license. On October 14, we switched planes and I began lessons in a Piper Aztec PA-23 6460Y, a fast twin-engine plane that was a delight to fly. After flying the much slower single-engine PA-28, it was a challenge to fly the twin, especially under actual instrument flying conditions. The instructor usually pulled an engine shortly after take-off, which made me work. When doing instrument flying, because of the increased speed, everything happened much faster and it kept me on my toes.

Around the Seattle area there is a lot of air traffic and while flying through the soup, often you are barely able to see your wing tips. The other aircraft were all around us, invisible in the clouds, and the pilots could be heard talking through the earphones.

On October 24, Frank Benedict, who was a designated FAA check pilot for the airline transport license, began giving me dual in preparation for the flying examination. Frank worked for Galvin's Flight Service but later went to work full time for the FAA at Boeing Field. He was a quiet, very competent, first-class instructor and a real gentleman.

Seven is my favorite number and good things in my life always seem to happen when a seven is involved. On December 7, 1970, Frank and I went up for the flight part of the examination for the ATP. I had already passed the written exam, the toughest I've ever taken, and I had to take it more than once to pass. When Frank and I were coming in to land at Boeing Field, after completing the rest of the exam in actual instrument conditions, we were doing an ILS (Instrument Landing System) approach and had clearance to land. Then an F-27 from an airline company cut in front of us and a voice came over my earphones, "Make an immediate left climbing turn," which I did and managed to avoid a crash. We circled and were coming in on the ILS again when this scene was repeated. These violations could have ended tragically for all of us and Frank said he was going to report it to the FAA.

After successfully making a third approach on the ILS and landing, Frank wrote in my pilot's log book: ATP passed, F. Benedict WE 15-32.

Frank told me the following: "Larry, you're the pilot in command. Always question any instruction the tower or anyone else gives to you and be sure it's a safe thing to do." He said that on three different occasions he would have killed himself if he did what the air traffic controller instructed him to do. I always remembered what Frank told me and I'm very careful to doublecheck and try to fly in a safe manner.

In the fall of 1973, Watson Lake Flying Service's accountant had purchased an Aztec PA-23 CF-HIA and leased it to the company. Because I was the only one who had flown an Aztec, I had the privilege of picking it up at Calgary, Alberta, and flying it to Watson Lake.

On October 11, 1973, I made my first flight with paying passengers into Fort Liard, Northwest Territories with the Aztec — a flight of 190 miles one way.

I did about 95 percent of all the flying in HIA that fall and during the flying seasons of 1974 and 1975. Instead of the normal 260-horsepower engines, it had the larger 290-horsepower Lycoming fuel-injected engines. It

A map of northern British Columbia and the Rocky Mountain trench.

was a beautiful airplane to fly and after flying the Beaver with an indicated air speed of 120 MPH, it was fun to cruise at 200 MPH IAS. It was like a Cadillac with its six thick, cushy seats.

In early June, 1975, I was checked out in the North American B-25 MWC at Watson Lake. This aircraft and another B-25, CF-OND, were used for water-bombing fires. I flew the B-25 CF-OND on a search and rescue mission, looking for a downed helicopter which we never found. F. L. Harold, Chief Pilot for Northwestern Air Lease, Ltd., certified my log book on June 15, 1975, and I had this type rating put on my Canadian commercial license. It's the same kind of bomber that Jimmy Doolittle used when he and several other pilots flew off a carrier and made the first bombing run on Japan in World War II. Whenever I hear of the Doolittle Raiders getting together, I think of that honest, high-performing B-25 with fondness. With its thick, high-lift wing, it gets airborne with a surprisingly short take-off run. It's a good, solid flying platform and fun to fly. Crawling up through a hatch in the belly, starting the powerful radial engines (1800-horsepower engines, I believe), listening to the engines' deep roar, and flying off in the Yukon skies are pleasant memories I have of the B-25.

We flew over high terrain north of Okanogan Lake and soon encountered lowering ceilings, which necessitated a turn toward the west, where the weather quickly improved to bright sunny skies and fewer clouds.

Douglas Lake appeared about twenty miles west, off our port wing. This lake is headquarters for Canada's largest cattle ranch, called the Douglas Lake Cattle Company. The ranch has over 160,000 deeded acres and has control of 350,000 acres of Crown grazing rights. The winter herd numbers about 11,000 head of cattle. When I visited a fishing lodge at Hatheume Lake, British Columbia, a year ago, one of the owners gave me a copy of a book called Cattle Ranch by Nina G. Woolliams, which tells the story of the Douglas Lake Cattle Ranch in vivid detail. A friend and I drove to Hatheume Lake, in the heart of this large cattle ranch, to watch some of the many loons that spend the summer there.

John Douglas, Sr., homesteaded on 320 acres by a lake he called Round Lake in the fall of 1872. He rode 100 miles to the magistrate's office in Lytton, B.C. on September 17, 1872, to record his half section and thus began the Douglas Lake Cattle Company. It has changed ownership many times since then.

Landed at Williams Lake at 1350. Ate lunch out of our grocery supply, on the grass in front of the William Lake Terminal.

We fueled up and then waited for favorable weather. After some three hours of waiting and checking the weather hourly at the FSS, we finally received a favorable report. Prince George was looking good and a few pilots had flown south down the Rocky Mountain Trench at 4,500 feet and reported good weather all the way. We decided to leave and stop for fuel at the town of Mackenzie near the southeast end of Williston Lake, then fly on to Watson Lake, where we planned to overnight. I filed a flight plan to Mackenzie, we climbed back into our ship, and I soon began writing in my journal:

1705: *Off Williams Lake, on course to Mackenzie, about 217 miles north.*

1734: *Rain at 7,333 feet, with good weather ahead and to the west, though some rain showers around. Hope to make Watson Lake by nightfall.*

1809: *Reported to Prince George radio on 126.7 our position. Changed flight plan to Watson Lake, going up trench, estimated time 3:30. At 8,000 feet, smooth, going to fuel up at Mackenzie and then go on. Like old times, feel so good. The country is full of clear-cut logging. The land has been raped.*

1850: *Landed at Mackenzie, where a pulp mill belches pollution a short distance west of the airport.*

1920: *Off Mackenzie on course to Watson Lake. First time I've flown the trench from Prince George to QH (Watson Lake). Following Williston Lake and can see why it's called the trench. Under the overcast ceiling it looks like a tunnel. Base of clouds about 5,500 feet and am at 4,920 feet. Broken cloud cover with some bright spots of sun shining through.*

Williston Lake looks like Puget Sound or the Inside Passage of British Columbia and Alaska. Huge lake, but the surrounding forests are badly clear-cut. This lake is about 143 miles long and an arm of the lake that extends east is over 60 miles long. This lake, formed by a dam, covers the lower portion of the Finlay River, and now creates electricity for the Province of British Columbia.

Blue sky above and off the starboard side of the nose. The rays of light shining over this great, vast land are truly beautiful. I feel like I'm home once again. Good tail wind. Smooth air and the light rays are like windows from heaven, with a surreal quality, like nothing I've ever experienced before.

I'm at complete peace with my world. I'm back home to a vast country with no habitation in sight, but logged-off areas can be seen. Whitecaps going my way. A great tail wind, indicating 105 knots at 5,270 feet.

1950: Rain, but sunshine ahead. Over the water with not many places to land except on the shore, and the engine seems to miss—just like in the old bush pilot days, when my ship and I were in the wilderness with no place to land, it seemed to miss.

1957: Tug below is pulling a large raft of logs heading south toward Mackenzie. It looks like a small toy. Mackenzie to Watson Lake is some 300 miles. This is truly my Northern Flight of Dreams. *The magnificent Rockies are just off our starboard wing and rise majestically above the shores of Williston Lake.*

2015: At 5,000 feet. The north end of Williston Lake is about three miles ahead. Janey is taking videos.

2023: Road and side roads run north and south from Fort Ware, B.C., an Indian village that was all wilderness in the late sixties when I flew the ski-shod Beaver to Fort Ware. It was March and I landed on the frozen waters of the Finlay River. It's sad to now see roads and clear-cuts close to where I parked the Beaver then.

On March 28, 1969, Mike Smith and Gene Winoski, from a company called IPEC, met me at McClure Lake. IPEC worked for B.C. Hydro, checking snow depth to determine water flow for the coming year. We flew in Omineca Air Service's Beaver CF-JOS on skis to Kaza Lake, Tsaydaychi Lake, and to Germansen Landing, British Columbia, where we overnighted at Westfall's place. Wes, as we called him, was originally from Sandpoint, Idaho. He and his wife manned a weather station for the government and were warm, gracious hosts whenever I stayed overnight. Wes had a Champ on floats and later purchased a Cessna 180 on floats. He flew off the river at Germansen Landing during the summer months. I understand Wes now winters in Arizona and spends summers with his wife on his brother's ranch

Larry Whitesitt standing in front of Omineca's Beaver ski plane CF-JOS, which he flew in March 1969 to Fort Ware with Mike Smith and Gene Winoski, who were from a company called IPEC..

near Sandpoint.

The following day, we flew to Tutizzi, Johanson, Frederickson and Pulpit lakes and then flew on to Fort Ware, where we overnighted at Art Van Sommer's home. Art was well-known and a living legend of the north. He freighted supplies for his store during the months when the Finlay River was open and sold his goods to the Indians at Fort Ware. During our stay, I had a chance to get acquainted.

Art talked slowly and easily and I could tell he was well-versed on the area, and of course on the Finlay River which provided his livelihood. He was a congenial host and my stay was enjoyable. He talked about Williston Lake and how it would affect things for him once it filled up. As I recall, Art was concerned about trees that might be left standing when it flooded and thought that it might be difficult to get a boat to shore. Where the Kenny Dam in British Columbia was built, it backs up some 250 miles of waterways, including Ootsa Lake. Trees were left standing and it was difficult or impossible in places for boats to get to shore.

Looking at the shoreline of Williston Lake as I flew over, it appeared that all the trees had been cut before it was flooded and an even, cleared shoreline could be seen. But the wild and free Finlay River is gone. It reminds me of the Columbia River that I knew as a boy, when the Indians fished for salmon at Celilo Falls in Washington state. Now those falls are also gone as a result of a dam. Actually, many dams have ruined the natural beauty of the great Columbia River and the once abundant salmon run. Again, British

Columbia let big business have their way.

On March 30, 1969, we departed Fort Ware. We landed on Sikanni, Chief and Lady Laurra lakes, Germansen Landing, and finally McClure Lake, our home base. Art is gone now, as is much of the Finlay River he loved and knew so well. As Fort Ware passed beneath our wings, I began to circle so Janey could get some good pictures. The Finlay River still runs by Fort Ware but a few miles south it runs into Williston Lake.

It seems so long ago, in another world, when I touched down below with the ski-equipped Beaver. It was a wilderness world then.

Fort Ware is an old Hudson Bay Post and is home to about 300 Sekani Indians, whose men are seasonal hunters and trappers by tradition. Food prices are some of the highest in British Columbia, so hunting greatly helps to keep down the cost of living. Moose, mountain goats, beaver, and rabbits are plentiful, and the fishing in the Finlay River is good.

About fifty children are taught school in the fall. Some of the children will see little of school, because they spend a good part of the year in trapline cabins with their families. The chief of the Fort Ware Band is Emil McCook. Some of the elders worry that logging and other traffic on the road will be bad for young people and affect the traditional hunting and trapping way of life. Before the roads, the Finlay River was the highway for these people.

I was sad as Fort Ware slipped behind and roads continued under our wings for many miles, but I remember another time when there was wilderness and those memories are precious.

2050: Roads are all gone and at last wilderness. Air smooth, wonderful clear air. A little later we're over Sifting Pass by Fox Lake, downhill to Watson Lake. Back in my country.

This area north to the Liard River just south of the Yukon border and west of the Alaska Highway to the Cassier Mountains is known as the Northern Rocky Mountain Wilderness Area. It is home to the grizzly bear, wolf, moose, deer, stone sheep, mountain goat, caribou, bald eagle, and loon, the voice of the wilderness.

Arctic rivers in this area are free-flowing, without dams, including the Kechika, which drains the Rocky Mountain Trench northwest from Sifton Pass into the Liard (sometimes referred to as the west branch of the Mackenzie), and the Mackenzie River itself. What geologists call the Rocky

Mountain Trench is 900 miles long, running in a northwest direction in the eastern part of British Columbia from the Montana border almost to the Liard River just south of the Yukon border.

Thutade Lake, southwest of our course about 55 miles, in the Stikine Plateau, is the headwaters of another arctic river, the Finlay. This lake, the shape of a crooked bow, is 27 miles long, about a mile wide, and 3,625 feet above sea level. The water from Thutade Lake must make a journey of some 2,362 miles before it meets saltwater at the Beaufort Sea. From Thutade Lake, the Finlay flows in a northeast direction, picking up the Firesteel River, which flows out of Tatlatuie Lake. It then heads north before making a large loop through the Cassiar Mountains eastward, picking up the Fox River south of Sifton Pass and becoming a river of the Trench, flowing southeast.

Long ago, the Finlay was joined by the Parsnip River at Finlay Forks, creating the Peace River, which then flowed eastward through the Rocky Mountains before it turned north. Because the Peace River is larger than either the Liard or Athabasca, the Finlay could be considered as the true head of Canada's longest River, the mighty MacKenzie River.

Now a dam spans the Peace River on the east side of the Rocky Mountains, just west of Hudson Hope. The reservoir is called Williston Lake and it covers the lower portion of the Finlay River.

In the late 1990s, a provincial parkland of 2.89 million acres was set aside in the Northern Rocky Mountains British Columbia's largest single designation of preserved wilderness. Because of the wide variety of large animals there, this region is sometimes called "the Serengeti of North America." Dr. Bruce McLellen, a noted grizzly bear biologist, said, "As far as large animal diversity and intact ecosystem goes, there's no place like the Northern Rockies outside Africa. It's a global treasure."

In 1959 I spent a honeymoon summer with my beautiful wife, Kathy, on a U.S. Forest Service lookout tower, Desert Lookout, in Montana's Rocky Mountains. Desert Lookout was a short distance south of the west entrance to Glacier National Park. That summer as I looked for the telltale signs of smoke, gazing north into the Canadian Rockies, I fell in love with the majestic Rocky Mountains. This affair of the heart has lasted a lifetime.

The following winter of 1960, our son, Scott, was born five minutes after our arrival at the Kalispel County Hospital, following a wild ride through the Rockies in a snowstorm, using our neighbor's car after I managed to get our blue 1953 Chevy firmly stuck in deep snow in our driveway. That summer I experienced the marvel of flight alone when I soloed beneath the peaks of the Rockies at the Kalispel County Airport in the sixty-five horsepower Taylor Craft that belonged to my instructor Jack Archibald.

In the 1960s and 1970s, I was most fortunate to be a bush pilot in Canada and had the wonderful experience of flying float planes and ski planes to rivers and lakes in this northern Rocky Mountain wilderness, often with my son, Scott, as copilot.

About 2115: *The weather ahead looks lousy. We're 110 miles from Watson Lake and the clouds are down to the ground, with the Rocky Mountain Trench plugged solid. We're about 15 or 20 miles south of Scoop Lake, as I turn east and try to go around the bad weather, about seven miles southeast of where the Gataga and Ketchika Rivers join. We fly over Netson Lake at 9:25 PM and follow Netson Creek to the Rabbit River, some 20 miles. The weather to the northeast is much better.*

I remembered flogging through similar weather many times in this country. It's like old times. My juices are flowing, the adrenalin is up and I'm concentrating on the map, looking for a safe port.

The tops of the mountains were clear of clouds to the northeast. If we couldn't make Watson Lake, it looked as if we could fly north to the Liard River Airstrip and spend the night there. I've flown off this strip in the past. I was concerned about finding a place where I could call and close my flight plan.

But the sky brightened in the direction of Watson Lake, which was northwest of our position by Graveyard Lake, so I banked left, flying just east of Graveyard and Gemini lakes. Janey didn't really appreciate it when, just after encountering some bad weather, I pointed out and told her, "That's Graveyard Lake." I chuckled to myself, but I think there was a grin on my face.

The Alaska Highway appeared by the north side of the Liard River and we could see that Watson Lake would be clear. What a marvelous feeling of relief and thanksgiving. The town of Watson Lake was named after the fur trader Frank Watson, who set up a post in the area during the 1890s. Watson Lake was founded with the construction of the airport in 1940. Airplanes that were flown to Russia on the Lend-Lease Program to help in the war effort stopped here for fuel. When the Alcan Highway was completed in 1942, businesses were established in Watson Lake to cater to the tourists who would eventually use the highway.

CHAPTER 8

Magic of the Yukon

Y ukon is an Indian name meaning "Greatest."

The Yukon Territory has 186,000 square miles and extends over 600 miles north, from the British Columbia border to the Arctic Ocean. From Alaska on the west border to the Northwest Territories to the east on its southern border measures some 583 miles. The Yukon population is about 35,000. The adjoining Northwest Territories has a population of approximately 91,000. The Yukon and Northwest Territories, both Canadian Territories, have 1,508,900 square miles, about three times the size of Alaska, or about the same size as the lower forty-eight United States.

As we neared Watson Lake, we were given the gift of a beautiful red sun just above the horizon beyond the airport. This brought memories of the last time I flew into Watson Lake in September 1989. At that time I received another gift, a marvelous display of the Northern Lights stretching across the heavens.

On 126.7, I pressed the mike button, "Watson Lake Radio, Cessna November 62731." I heard a faint voice and repeated my call.

"Cessna 62731, this is Whitehorse Radio."

"Roger, I'm inbound for the airport, landing in ten minutes."

They gave me the wind and altimeter setting and advised me to turn to 122.3, the frequency local traffic at Watson Lake uses. Watson Lake no longer has a Flight Service Station, I learned, but Whitehorse has a Repeater Station there and the reception is good. Whitehorse Radio advised me to close my flight plan on 126.7 after I landed. We touched down just before dark and

I closed my flight plan with Whitehorse Radio.

We taxied to Watson Lake Flying Service's fuel pump, located about fifty feet south of their hanger. It was such a good feeling to be back in the Yukon. I pulled the fuel mixture to the full lean position and the engine quickly stopped. Switches of, master off, and we had silence. The Yukon is a magic land and this was a special time for me.

I walked to the nearby hanger where I could see men working on airplanes. I asked them if I could get fuel.

"Oh, not this late, unless you want to pay an extra fee."

"Not really. Say, I used to fly the Red Beaver. My name is Larry Whitesitt."

"Oh, I've read your book. I think we can get you some fuel with no extra charge."

"Thanks."

The engineer's sister appeared and walked with me over to the gas shack; she turned on the pump and I pushed a platform on wheels under the wing, then climbed up and topped both tanks.

"Thanks for your help. By the way, we need a lift."

"I'll call a cab for you."

Shortly after I tied down my ship, the cab arrived and we drove south toward town. The airport and the actual Watson Lake by the airport are five miles from the town of Watson Lake.

I asked the driver if he could take us to the Watson Lake Flying Service's float plane dock. He agreed, we turned right off the paved road, and drove down a gravel road to a dock.

There in bright new red plumage sat my favorite ship of all time, the Red Beaver CF-IBP. I walked down a ramp and across the familiar dock and gave IBP a hug around the strut, as I felt tears in my eyes. It was wonderful to see that magnificent, faithful ship once again. After a silent time of fond memories, I walked back to the taxi and we drove toward the Belvedere Hotel, where we were able to book a room.

The taxi cab driver a friendly, congenial fellow, helped us unload our baggage and carry it into the hotel. We put it down in front of the lobby desk as a familiar-looking, pretty young woman greeted us.

The young woman said her name was Dawn Thibaudeau and she looked so much like her mother, Lynn, whom I had known when I flew at Watson Lake. Lynn was married to Jim Thibaudeau, a Bush Pilot, with whom I flew at B.C. Yukon Air Service and at Watson Lake Flying Service. Jim was killed in a flying accident in October 1975, after encountering severe icing conditions in Northern British Columbia about forty miles south of Watson Lake.

We had a friendly talk and a little later when I came back to the lobby, Dawn said, "Mom is on the phone. She's at the Watson Lake Hotel."

"Fine. I'd like to talk to her."

I took the phone and said, "Lynn, would you wait until I can freshen up and I'll join you?"

"Yes, but I can only stay for a short while, as we have to get home soon."

"I'll be there. I hope you can wait."

After a shower, Janey and I walked down the familiar Main Street that's the Alaska Highway, and then down a side street to the Watson Lake Hotel. As I walked through the door of the familiar log Watson Lake Hotel Lounge, Lynn greeted me with a smile. She was sitting with her husband, Bill Ellis, whom she introduced, another couple, and a single man, all sitting at the same table near the door.

Lynn and I had a lively catch-up conversation, while her husband and Janey had a dance. Lynn looked as young as I remembered her when she and Jim Thibaudeau were dating in 1969. Jim and I worked together at B.C. Yukon Air Service that year. We talked and talked. Janey and I each had a Poose Capay, a local drink with seven different liqueurs that has a good kick.

A married woman at our table began talking about Indian culture and some of their beliefs. She said the owl was a sign of death to the Indians. I told her about the brilliant white "Spirit Owl" I saw outside the window of my room when I stayed overnight at the Old Hudson Bay Store in Telegraph Creek. It was Saturday, September 9, 1989, and I was sleeping in one of the old storerooms behind the main store, which is now privately owned and is called the River Song Inn. Something woke me at about 0400, I sat up in bed and looked outside. I saw an owl suspended in air, not moving. It gave me an intense look--a look of warning, not a threatening stare. After a time, the owl floated sideways towards the east, and disappeared from my window view.

On that trip, I had planned to leave early in the morning and fly back to Spokane that day, although I was extremely fatigued after long hours of flying and little sleep. But I took the Spirit Owl as a warning and decided to sleep in, which I did. Also, one of Fletcher Day's guides had drowned in a

Janey Youngblood and Larry met Lynn Ellis and her husband at the Watson Lake Hotel in the summer of 1993 and reminisced about the past.

wilderness lake and they were having his funeral at noon on that Saturday.

This experience at Telegraph Creek now had new meaning and I was glad I had heeded the owl's warning and rested before flying to Spokane.

Lynn invited us to a housewarming at their new log home on Watson Lake the following evening.

Lynn works for the Royal Canadian Mounted Police and had to make an appearance in the morning so she excused herself and we said good night. As we walked out the door of that special place, the memories of long-ago friends flooded my mind. I remembered the many good times spent telling tales and drinking Poose Capays with my fellow Bush Pilots and outfitters.

Friday morning 0632: *I'm back in the Yukon, where this far north journey began. The wonderful Yukon flying adventure and all the great people who touched my life here. As we walked down Main Street, Janey took videos, slides and prints of the town.*

0738: *Watson Lake Hotel, drinking coffee with Janey. We're sitting in a corner at a round table. The log beams supporting the second story are dark brown and I feel like I'm sitting in a unique place of history. A chunky, cute Indian baby is entertaining the guests here. Sun's shining. Think maybe we will stay here another night and maybe go to Lynn's new log home housewarming party tonight.*

0805: *An Indian couple are sitting a few tables away. They're in their*

Janey Youngblood stands in front of Watson Lake Flying Service's Cessna 185 CF YIG.

thirties, I think. Now a group of three Indian women and their men have joined them at the same table. I talked to Doug Brown, whom I knew from my bush pilot days at Watson Lake, and he gave me his card. It read "Francis River Construction, Ltd., Box 274, Watson Lake, Yukon YOA 1CO." Doug was always quick to tell a humorous story and had a terrific sense of humor. He could see the funny side of an otherwise serious situation. I like Doug.

We hired a taxi and at 0940, we stopped to see Lynn at the Royal Canadian Mounted Police Station where she has worked for several years. Janey took some pictures of Lynn and me.

We arrived at the Watson Lake Flying Service Seaplane Base shortly after 1000 and Janey began filming the loading and unloading of the float planes that arrived and departed. She took pictures of a loon swimming a few hundred feet south of the float plane dock. I miss those days when I was a bush pilot and could listen to the haunting calls of loons on Watson Lake. They were the first birds to arrive in the spring. They live twenty years or more, and perhaps this loon we saw was one that I had seen when I taxied out on the lake in the Red Beaver.

We had a nice visit with Bob Close, who was in the office talking on the radio to a company pilot and to the outfitters in the bush. Bob helps run the office, as well as holding his full-time job with the Yukon government.

(From left to right) Pilots Dave, Jim Thibaudeau, Stan Bridcut, Larry, Jim Close, John Poizer and Wally Waulkonan (kneeling in front) pose in front of a Beech 18 CF-NCL. Jim Thibaudeau was killed in this plane, along with two hunters, in the fall of 1975 after encountering severe icing about 40 miles south of Watson Lake.

He is a very pleasant, conscientious young man whom I respect highly. I remember so well those years when I flew for Watson Lake Flying Service. At that time, it was Jim Close, Bob's father, who was on the radio talking to me as I flew the Red Beaver in the bush.

Jim Close and Stan Bridcut still own and operate Watson Lake Flying Service; this company is the oldest in the Yukon still owned by the original group. Bob appears to be more involved in the running of the company and in addition to operating the radio he takes care of the books. When I first started flying out of Watson Lake, Bob and my son, Scott, were just boys. Now they are both young men with careers of their own. It was nice to see that Bob, like his father, was also a pilot and involved in the company's daily operation.

I remember how hard Jim Close worked when I flew for Watson Lake Flying Service. From early morning until late at night during the busy flying season, he operated the radio and expedited for the outfitters. A top-notch engineer, he also did a lot of the mechanical and airframe work on the planes. Jim, who was born in the Yukon and spent his entire life in this magic land, still continued his many roles, but now he had Bob's help. Stan, Jim's partner, continued to do some of the flying, much as he did when I worked for the company. He also did some of the expediting.

In 1987, I visited Watson Lake Flying Service and went on a flight in the company's Cessna 185 float plane, CF-YIG, with a pilot named Paul Stahnke. We flew with two Germans to Clark Lake, Northwest Territories, where we left them. They were going to float down the outlet of Clark Lake and then down the South Nahanni River. We flew to Don Taylor's Stewart Lake Lodge and then Paul let me fly the leg back to Watson Lake.

When I asked Paul about his flying in the Yukon and what he might have learned here, as opposed to the flying he did commercially on the coast of British Columbia, he replied, "When I flew for Stan and Jimmy, I learned some important things. Only one of these seemed to be about flying. I learned how to handle myself with river work. That is something we don't have on the coast. The basic lesson was the value of people."

He gave an illustration about a client of theirs who didn't have any money. They just kept flying for him, even though his bill was quite high. Paul said, "They consider it almost a duty to operate this way, and the trappers and other customers in the Bush without money are treated in the same manner. It's like they're an institution, and maybe because they're businessmen second. In the north, they outlasted everyone. Sometimes nice guys do finish first, and they earned it."

Janey's video camera was busy recording the Red Beaver as it landed on the lake, taxied to the dock, and loaded for another flight into the bush. That wonderful sound of the 450 Pratt and Whitney R-985, nine-cylinder radial engine was recorded as the Red Beaver started, belched blue smoke, and taxied away from the dock. She looked fine in her new bright red coat of paint — the red de Havilland Beaver that, for many years, was my close and faithful companion as we flew together over a vast wilderness in Northern British Columbia, Yukon and Northwest Territories. She never let me down and safely carried me over thousands of miles across that rugged terrain. She looked beautiful as she carried a huge pile of gear and three hunters who were flying to an outfitter's hunting camp. I had a strange, sad feeling that this would be the last time that I would see the Red Beaver.

Janey recorded the Red Beaver on video as the plane taxied away from the dock, and a short time later roared by during the take-off run and disappeared behind a point of land. A short time later I watched the Red Beaver, a small speck flying south toward the British Columbia border. "So long, my friend."

We walked up the gravel road to the Campbell Highway to get a picture of the Watson Lake Flying Service's sign. We passed a man parking a long camper trailer pulled behind a pickup. After we had taken the pictures and begun walking back toward the base, the man came out of the trailer that was now parked near some trees and said, "Larry, I thought that was you."

It was Johnny Drift and his wife, Marianne, from Williams Lake, British Columbia.

"Come on in, it's good to see you folks."

"I've been keeping track of you, Johnny. You were operating a guiding service out of Kluane Lake."

"Yes, but I sold that outfit and now I really miss the guiding business. We sold the business because Marianne was ill and we didn't think she would live long. So we travelled a lot and did things we wanted, but didn't have time to do before. Now Marianne is in good health and we miss being in the bush."

We visited and talked about the old days when Johnny and his wife ran an excellent hunting camp out of Burnt Rose Lake, near the Turnigan River in British Columbia about eighty miles south of Watson Lake. They built a beautiful log lodge. The notching and concaving of the logs in their lodge was similar to the construction of our former log home near Smithers, British Columbia in the Driftwood Valley. They treated their hunters to first-class accommodations and an excellent hunt.

The outfitter who had purchased Johnny's hunting territory offered me a ride to the airport, so Johnny and Marianne walked Janey and me down the hill to the float plane base. Janey took photos of Johnny, Marianne, and myself leaning against a Piper Super Cub on floats that was pulled up on shore. Johnny flies his own Super Cub. They invited me to visit them at Williams Lake where they have built a log home. I felt that if nothing else was accomplished on this flight, seeing and visiting with the Drifts once again was worth this flight north.

Jim Close was now at the base after returning from town and we had a pleasant visit. Jim and I discussed a flight to the Nahanni country that I was contemplating. Jim and Bob offered to give me some aviation gas that they had at Cantung in the Northwest Territories, if I decided to fly in the Nahanni country, since fuel is hard to find up there.

I walked outside to help Stan Bridcut push off from the dock in the Cessna 185 CF-YIG. I held onto the tail until he started the engine and then taxied south into the deeper waters of the lake.

A short time before, Stan weighed the hunter, who was quite large and probably in his sixties. Stan apologized but said he had to weigh him and his gear, as they were restricted on how much they could haul.

The hunter laughed and replied, "At my age it doesn't bother me to get weighed."

Stan looked much the same, but wore glasses now. He remained lean, still had a sly sense of humor, an easy grin and quiet manner. He was still agile and I watched him climb up on the wing like a youngster as he fueled the plane.

It was time to go and I said goodbye to Jim and Bob. Then the outfitter drove us to the airport.

CHAPTER 9

Flight to Dawson City

After running a preflight check and loading our gear inside, we climbed aboard. We had decided to fly to Dawson City and I had called Whitehorse and filed a flight plan. We lifted off runway 26 after advising local traffic on 123.2 of our intentions. In the air, I notified Whitehorse radio on 126.7 that we were airborne and we opened our flight plan.

The weather was sunny with scattered cumulus clouds overhead. I almost called Whitehorse radio to change my flight plan to Fort Liard and fly over Virginia Falls and Deadmen Valley on the Nahanni, but decided to go to Dawson City and then north to Old Crow and the Yukon Arctic coastline, which I had never seen.

As we headed northwest toward Ross River where I planned to refuel, Simpson, Sambo, and Hasselberg lakes passed beneath our starboard wing to the north. It was familiar country and it felt good, comfortable, to fly over the wilderness again. Here, I can breathe, see beautiful country, and probably not see another airplane for hundreds of miles. I always feel much more at ease, the farther I am from airports and human restrictions that take away much of the joy of flight! We followed the Liard River for a time, to its headwaters and beyond.

1443: Beautiful, restful country. "I'm at home, Lars." I call myself Lars at times — when I write and when I think. Ross River seems such a long way and I question my navigation skills, but eventually it appears where it's supposed to be. The last time I was here was in 1975, I believe,

when I flew for Watson Lake Flying Service. I called my position and
intentions to land on the local traffic frequency of 122.1 for Ross River,
but all I heard was silence on the radio. Flying over the airport, I could
tell by the wind sock that there was a very strong wind from the west.

The gravel runway at Ross River is 5,500 feet long and the elevation is 2,314 feet. We landed on runway 26, as there was a very strong, gusty wind out of the northwest. I used a phone at a helicopter office on the field to call the fuel man, and learned that I would have to buy a full 45-gallon drum of AV gas.

"But I only need about twenty gallons."

"Sorry, but that's the only way we sell fuel here."

I discussed my problem with the helicopter engineer and the pilot, who made some phone calls.

"You can get fuel at Mayo. You have to call the Whitepass Office when you land and he will drive to the airport."

"Thank you for your help."

When I mentioned my name and that I once worked for Watson Lake Flying Service, the pilot said, "Oh, I've read your book, *Flight of the Red Beaver.*"

"I guess I'll fly to Mayo and fuel up there. So long and thanks."

We lifted off runway 26 and flew a heading of 284° to Mayo.

My son, Scott, and I flew this route in a twin engine Aztec CF-HIA for Watson Lake Flying Service in 1975. We flew two mining officials from Tungsten (called Cantung) to Dawson City and overnighted there at Black Mike's Hotel, an original left over from the Gold Rush days. The following day, we flew these men to a mining camp west of Dawson City and then to Whitehorse, where they caught a plane.

Scott was such a good, cheerful companion and I cherish those summers we flew together out of Watson Lake. He was a good copilot and often I let him fly. Scott pumped the floats, cleaned out the airplane, and helped me load. Those were great days and I have many fond memories. Scott recently told me, "Dad, when you gave me the controls and let me fly, I was scared but I wouldn't let you know!"

We flew over Swim Lake, twenty-two miles out of Ross River, and sixty miles farther west over a larger lake called Earn Lake, and then thirty miles later we sighted Big Kalzas Lake. Mayo was only forty miles away.

A woman's voice came over my headset, "Mayo radio will be off the air for five minutes while I check the weather station."

I tried to call her on 122.1 as I was about ten minutes out, but received no response.

The wind was gusty as I circled the airport and the dancing windsock showed the direction of the wind was from the west. We landed on runway 24, a gravel strip with loose rocks. After taxiing to a fuel pump and shutting down the engine, I phoned the fuel man from a nearby pay phone.

We sat down on a few blades of grass and had a picnic of sorts, eating some of our survival food, including some dried apricots. After waiting about a half hour, an older gentleman arrived and opened the fuel shack. I pulled out the hose and topped both tanks. Besides the cost of the fuel, there was an additional fifteen-dollar service charge, but I was just glad to get fuel.

After fueling, I walked to the Flight Service Station and talked to the woman radio operator.

"Oh, I didn't know you landed."

"Well, I called you just after you said you were going off the air to check the weather, but missed you."

We were much closer to our destination of Dawson City, which was about 100 miles west. The Mayo Airport is a bit north of the Stewart River, where the town of Mayo is located.

Once in our plane, I called Mayo Radio and the woman gave the wind, which favored runway 24, and the altimeter setting. We lifted off at 2005 on course to Dawson City.

When I was a boy, I listened to Sergeant Preston of the Canadian Northwest Mounted Police on a weekly radio program. Sergeant Preston and his faithful sled dog, King, were always in pursuit of a criminal, in weather most foul, and a raging blizzard could be heard almost drowning out the good Sergeant's yell, "Mush you huskies, mush—onward King—onward." I dreamed of one day going to that magic land. Reading Jack London's Call of the Wild, a story of a dog named Buck cruelly treated with severe beatings, working as a sled dog, who eventually escapes and lives wild and free in the wilderness, my boyhood imagination ran wild as I dreamed of a wilderness experience someday.

We flew just south of Minto Lake, some ten miles west of Mayo and crossed the McQueston River north of the abandoned community of McQueston, about 65 miles southeast of Dawson City.

2031: *Quiet, peaceful country. The valley going into Dawson is up ahead.*

About twenty miles east and a little south of Dawson, we flew over the Klondike River, which parallels the road that goes by the airport and on to Dawson. The Klondike River joins the Yukon River at the edge of Dawson City.

The Klondike Gold Rush began August 17, 1896, when gold was discovered on Rabbit Creek (later named Bonanza) by George Carmack and his two Indian friends, Tagish Charlie and Skookum Jim. This gold rush was one of the most incredible ones the world has ever known. Within days of this discovery, all the Klondike River tributaries were alive with the sound of gold miners hurriedly seeking their fortunes. But it wasn't until the summer of 1897, when the new millionaires from the Klondike were unloading their two tons of gold from the S.S. Excelsior in Seattle and the S.S. Portland in San Francisco, that the news of the Klondike Gold Rush flashed around the world.

Probably over 100,000 people started out for the Klondike, including the mayor of Seattle, but only some 40,000 actually made it. The dream and the reality upon arriving were two different things! Dawson City was rapidly changed from a canvas tent and log cabin boomtown to the largest city west of Winnipeg and north of San Francisco. By the turn of the century, Dawson was a refined city with many stately homes and impressive government buildings with running water, electricity and telephones.

Gold mining has been revived due to the high price of gold and the more efficient machines that can go through old mine tailings and extract the gold that was missed.

At latitude 64°, Dawson is only 159 miles south of the Arctic Circle and has almost continuous daylight in June and July. The hills are alive with over a hundred varieties of wild flowers and many birds and wildlife.

Twenty-five miles from Dawson is the beginning of the Dempster Highway, which goes northeast through the Richardson and Ogilvie Mountain Ranges to the MacKenzie River Delta, some 10,000 square miles of waterways and wetlands, and into Inuvik Northwest Territories.

I called Dawson City Radio on 126.7 when I was about twenty miles east. The wind was favoring runway 20. Dawson City Airport has a 5,000 foot gravel strip at an elevation of 1,214 feet.

Larry standing next to his plane after landing at Dawson City.

We landed on runway 20 and tied our ship to some buckets filled with rocks. I don't like to leave a plane, especially overnight, without tying it securely. The strong wind can easily move a small airplane, even with the brakes on.

I'm sitting on the grass at the Dawson City Airport. It's 2207 and my friend and I are waiting for a cab at the airport. We are now at the destination of the Klondikers in 1896-1899.

After several phone calls to various inns, Janey contacted the Dawson City Bed and Breakfast Inn and the owner, Jon Magnusson, said he would drive out to get us. The airport is ten miles east of town and after a short wait, Jon arrived. About halfway to town, I remembered my books and brochures that were left in the plane.

"Could you please go back? I have a book I want to promote and I've left it in the plane."

Jon was nice enough to accommodate me. We arrived at the Dawson City Bed and Breakfast, a two-story, quaint and very clean home, about 2230.

2250: Sitting on the bed at Dawson City Bed and Breakfast. The view of the Yukon River is quite spectacular and a breeze through the window feels great. It's a rugged land that the gold-seekers found here. Of course, now it's a tourist attraction and that's just fine, Lars. I would like to get up to Old Crow tomorrow and then fly to the nearby Arctic

A picture of Dawson City taken from a nearby hill.

Ocean.

We left the bed and breakfast establishment after a shower and walked along the Yukon River toward downtown.

2417: *Sitting on the bank of the Yukon River. It's quiet and peaceful here. We walked to the Midnight Sun Hotel Restaurant and had dinner. Then we returned to our two-story home for a much-needed sleep.*

0135: *I'm sitting on the balcony. A few drops of rain and a cool breeze feel good. The Yukon River is a few hundred feet away. It's nice to be here, but it's nice to think of home, also.*

Saturday July 31, 1993, Dawson City

0727: *Looking out the window of the small but comfortable room at the Klondike River where it joins the Yukon River about 100 yards west.*

We ate a delicious breakfast and then walked to the bank of the Klondike River, taking pictures and commenting on how clear it is, until it

The S.S. Keno is a large paddle-wheeler built in 1922 by the British Yukon Navigation Company and used on the Yukon River.

joins the silty-looking Yukon River. A sign along the bank, close to where the clean Klondike river enters the muddy Yukon reads:

Klondike River: The Klondike River flows southwest from the Ogilvie Mountains, meeting the Yukon River at Dawson City. The word Klondike is adapted from an Indian word meaning Hammer Water, describing the posts that were driven into the river bed to form salmon traps. Until the late 19th century, the river was noted only for its abundant fish, but then gold was discovered on its tributary, Bonanza Creek. The area was transformed. By 1889, all the important creeks in the district were staked and the word Klondike had become synonymous with wealth and abundance.

At 0954, I was looking at the S.S. Keno, a large paddle-wheeler built in 1922 by the British Yukon Navigation Company. At 1000, I called the Flight Service Station at the airport — the weather report at Dawson and Old Crow was good.

1040: Feel great, sitting on a large rock near the ferry crossing at the end of town. Cars are lined up for a block and the ferry is on the other side of the river. Think we may go to the Arctic today. The ferry's backing off. A couple from Italy are standing by their car, a few feet away, waiting for the ferry. Weather is good, "high overcast." On the other side of the river is the Top-Of-The-World Highway that goes to Alaska.

Various historical buildings, including the newer school that is built in the style of the Gold Rush era, were recorded on film when we walked through town. .

We walked up to Robert Service's cabin and a gentleman with a distinct strong Scottish accent was talking about the cabin and the deep meaning it had, and then he quoted the poem Robert Service wrote about his beloved cabin, aptly called "Goodbye, Little Cabin."

Jack London, the author, lived for a short time in Dawson City during that wild summer of 1898 and his cabin on Henderson Creek has been moved into Dawson.

After we listened to the poem, which really had a wonderful message of the bond Robert Service had to his Yukon cabin, much like I did to my northern cabin, we returned to our temporary Dawson City two-story home. Jon Magnusson told us he met Inday, his Oriental wife from Hong Kong, through correspondence.

He said, "We both traveled extensively before we married, so we really enjoy being in one place. We spend a lot of time working on our home." They are an attractive couple and have a well-run establishment. It was cozy, very clean, and the breakfast was delicious!

After taking some pictures of Jon and Inday and ourselves in front of their Dawson City Bed and Breakfast Inn, Jon took us back to the airport. On the way, we watched some A-26 World War II bombers, now used for dropping water on fires. At the airport, Janey took pictures of these impressive, noisy bombers taking off and landing.

The weather report said a front had moved in between Dawson and Old Crow, bringing bad conditions, so we decided to return to Watson Lake, then fly to the South Nahanni River in the Northwest Territories and take pictures of Virginia Falls and Deadmen Valley.

After topping the tanks, doing a thorough preflight inspection of the aircraft, and filing a flight plan, we left the land of the Klondike around 1300. We landed at Mayo for fuel and at 1507, we were airborne again on course to Watson Lake.

1533: *7,000 feet, on a heading of 110° on course to QH (Watson Lake) over McMillan River. Earn Lake is up ahead.*

1552: *Over Toy River.*

1646: *Finlayson Lake, five miles northeast of position. Frances Lake will soon be in sight. That's where I almost had to land in the lake with a Beaver that was on wheels. It was bad weather, nearly dark, and I was almost out of gas. At 1703, we flew near Frances Lake.*

I remember that day well. It was early July, 1975, when I thought the Beaver and I would have to land on the east arm of Frances Lake. Earlier that day I flew to Macmillan Pass Airstrip, north of Frances Lake, near the Yukon, Northwest Territory border, with some gear for a mining company. The weather had been bad most of the day, but lifted in the afternoon and I made the flight to the McMillan Pass strip, but when I was just south of Frances Lake on the way home, the weather closed in and extended to the ground. When I turned back, it had closed in to the north and I could only fly to the east arm of the lake.

Almost out of gas, the needles for the three gas tank gauges bouncing off empty, and with darkness descending, I decided to either land on the lake or in the trees by a cabin where a young couple lived. I had flown this couple, who were originally from the United States, in a seaplane before. They would come into town from their wilderness home once a year to work for a few weeks in order to buy flour, sugar, and staples. Then for the rest of the year, they would fish with nets and hunt for the meat they needed for themselves and their dogs.

Well, when things looked about as bad as they could get, I saw a bit of light in a saddle between two mountain peaks and I was able to sneak over the ridge and land on the Campbell Highway, which was a gravel road. I figured it was a one-chance shot, as it was now quite dark and the gas tanks were almost empty. With full flaps and fortunately landing slightly uphill, I didn't have to use brakes, which on that narrow stretch could have caused us to go down a bank and wreck the plane.

I was so happy and relieved to be safely on the ground, with body, soul, and airplane in one piece, that I didn't care if I ever flew again. I had to taxi for about two miles with my landing lights on so I could see the road, until I found a place where I could pull off and sleep.

The following morning, the horror of almost having to crash the previous night was mostly forgotten and I was ready to fly off on a new adventure. I walked down to a bay on the west arm of Frances Lake out of which Jim Thibaudeau was flying his favorite airplane, the float-equipped Beech 18 CF NCL. He was flying freight for an outfitter named Lori Bliss to a hunting camp in the Northwest Territories where he guided. We loaded a drum of AV gas in a pickup and drove to the Beaver. After fueling the plane, Jim went down the road in one direction and another man went in the opposite direction to flag down any vehicles that might be coming through. I took off and flew the Beaver back to Watson Lake. Jim and Stan, the owners of Watson Lake Flying Service were wondering what had happened to me, as I was supposed to be back the day before.

This was my first time back this way since I quit flying the bush for Watson Lake Flying Service in 1975 and the memories were many.

August 30, 1974: *Almost wrecked the Aztec. Today was another grey hair day, one of my most nerve-racking. I flew to Macmillan Pass with my son, Scott, to pick up a load of mining gear. The strip was fifteen hundred to two thousand feet long and forty-five hundred feet above sea level. Fortunately, after putting in a heavy payload, I had the sense to unload a few heavy items. This was after warming up, taxiing for take-off, and then deciding not to take an unnecessary risk. Good thinking for me this day! No doubt saved a wrecked airplane and possibly our lives!*

After unloading the heavy items that were on top, I taxied to the far north end of the gravel strip. I applied full power, released the brakes, and picked up speed rapidly as the two powerful engines propelled us toward the end of the strip. Just as I began to rotate past the point of no return, the door popped open. Not having room to stop, and knowing I would go off the end of the strip if we didn't become airborne, I somehow managed to lift the plane into the air.

The flight manual says if the door comes open in a situation like this, the outcome is "doubtful"— or words to that effect. We staggered into the air and down the valley. Bringing up the landing gear helped somewhat, but we struggled down the valley for many miles until I got some altitude and could breathe regularly. Scott was holding onto the door for dear life, pulling it as far shut as he could, but the air pressure kept it from closing completely. The airplane continued to buck and complain all the way home.

During the flying season of 1974 and 1975 I flew into Howard's Pass, about 100 miles northeast of Frances Lake. I call this my white knuckle strip. It was the toughest strip I ever flew into on a regular basis and it's probably one of the reasons I got out of flying the bush when I did.

On a typical trip into the strip at Howard's Pass, I was carrying explosives on the Beaver. As usual, a crosswind was coming down the mountain, tending to push me off the strip into a draw. As I bounced around the curve, the wind and centrifugal force and the sloping strip pushed me toward the draw. I bounced to the very edge and rode the ridge along the drop-off! Full left aileron, left rudder and we somehow stayed on the edge until the plane slowed. At that time, I got it back on the main strip, but I mentally expected a wreck and an explosion at any moment. I once made four passes at that strip before landing.

Frances River begins at the south end of the lake, where the east and west arms join, and we followed the road that parallels this river. About seventeen miles northwest of the Watson Lake Airport, the Frances River enters the Liard River. About forty miles north of Watson Lake, we flew near Simpson Lake, and just over fifteen miles east of there is Stewart Lake, where Don Taylor lives with his new bride. Don has a beautiful wilderness lodge with fishing cabins.

The last time I visited with Don was in 1987, when I flew as a passenger in Watson Lake Flying Service's Cessna 185 YIG and we landed at Stewart Lake. Don had just made some fresh peanut butter cookies and we had a nice visit. A loon on the lake near the front of the lodge stuck out its chest and flapped its wings. The fishing for red trout was very good, as I recall. The meat is red, I was told, because of the abundant fresh water shrimp the trout eat. Paul Stahnke, the pilot, let me fly YIG from Stewart Lake back to Watson Lake, which I thoroughly enjoyed.

We flew east of the airport and over the Watson Lake Flying Service Float Plane Base, taking pictures, and then landed into the wind on runway 26. Stan Bridcut drove up to the fuel shack to see if I needed anything after he watched us fly over the base. We had a short friendly conversation and topped the tanks. Stan has a quick friendly smile and a good sense of humor.

CHAPTER 10

Spirits of Deadmen Valley

I filed a new flight plan to Nahanni Butte, where we planned to camp for the night, and said goodbye to Stan. After starting up and taxiing toward the runway, I remembered I hadn't drained fuel from the tanks to check for water and contamination. I stopped the engine and drained some fuel into a clear plastic container and the gas looked free of any contamination. I went through my familiar checklist, CIGFTPR (Controls, Instruments, Gas, Flaps, Trim, Prop, Run-up), which I use along with the normal checklist of the airplane I'm flying. GUMP (Gas, Undercarriage, Mixture, Prop) is a standard precheck list I use before landing that covers the basics in addition to the checklist of the airplane. Using these checklists helps me to cover the basics for a safe flight and to not forget something important.

I remember well the day I began using the Beaver that I flew for B.C. Yukon Air Service in the summer of 1970, for water bombing a fire that was threatening to burn the town of Watson Lake. After the engineer installed the two ninety-gallon water tanks, one on top of each float, the senior pilot in charge decided to make the first water drop on the fire. I sat in the right copilot's seat while he flew. After applying full throttle and getting on the step (the planing position) and filling the water tanks, the engine quit just before lift-off. He forgot to switch to the fullest gas tank for take-off. Another minute and we could have crashed in the trees. A bomber from World War II sits at the bottom of Watson Lake because the pilot took off on a tank that was empty, except for enough fumes to get him airborne. That is one very good reason for having a good checklist that a pilot should follow

145

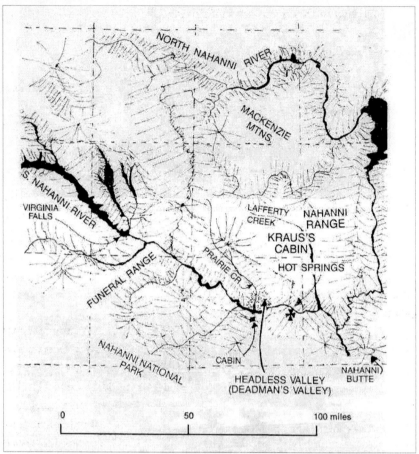

This is a map showing the location of Virginia Falls and Deadmen Valley (or Headless Valley).

consistently before take-off and before landing.

We lifted off runway 26 on course to Virginia Falls, Deadmen Valley, and the Indian village of Nahanni Butte. Heading northeast, we flew over some hills and then followed the Hyland River that is in the first valley east of Watson Lake.

1848: 5,900 feet. Quartz Lake is off starboard wing. Been there many times and once flew the Beeche 18 CF-NCL there. Hyland River is off port wing. We're starting to follow the Green River on a northeasterly direction to the fabled Nahanni River.

BACK HOME

Air is smooth at 5,800 feet; about 6,200 feet there is bad turbulence near cloud base. Just passed over Coal River. We're heading for Seaplane Lake and it's like old times. We followed the Coal River about 20 miles northwest and flew by two small lakes.

We crossed a ridge a mile east of two lakes, about eight miles east of the Coal River, and entered the Northwest Territories, some fifty air miles southwest of Virginia Falls. I flew just a few miles east of Seaplane Lake where I once landed a float plane in the early 1970s, fifteen miles northeast of the border. Seaplane Lake drains into the Flat River, which runs in an easterly direction about ten miles, then turns north for a short distance before making a 90° turn east, and some forty miles later enters the South Nahanni River.

I headed north to Flat Creek, east of Irwin Creek, flew through a pass, then dropped low over the South Nahanni River, about twenty miles north of the Flat River. I wanted to fly over the Nahanni for several miles downstream to Virginia Falls to get a feel for the country again, and to fly over the falls. As we dropped low between the bare peaks of the mighty Mackenzie Mountains, I felt that I was flying into a forbidden place. I remembered the times flying in the Nahanni country when I didn't know if I would survive to fly another day. The sky was overcast and the late afternoon was gray as an ominous feeling of danger filled the cockpit.

On a small lake, not much more than a pond, I dove low so we could fly close to two moose to get pictures. Then I followed the green, familiar winding river and remembered the many adventures experienced in the Nahanni when I flew here as a Bush Pilot in the Red Beaver.

The dangerous Nahanni is said to be the fastest river in North America and has been known to rise seven feet in an hour after one of the common, but vicious, rain and wind storms that pass through.

About fifty miles downstream we viewed an awesome and unforgettable sight as the river dropped away from us and plunged downward at the place called Virginia Falls. I circled several times so Janey could get videos, slides,

This is a view of Virginia Falls from Larry's airplane. Larry (inset picture) is sitting at the top of the falls, which is twice as high as Niagra Falls. "One of God's awesome wonders," Larry says.

and prints. Just a few hundred yards above the falls, on the south bank, is a grassy spot where I used to tie up the Red Beaver. It looked so close to the falls now. If the engine had quit on the Beaver, it could have been a wild ride over the falls, but the reliable plane never let me down.

It was at this place in 1971 that Scott and I had landed in the Red Beaver. On that rainy day, our passengers were a park supervisor and his helpers, a young man and woman. They were mapping out future campsites for this area, which later became the Nahanni National Park. With my trusty Argus C-3 camera, I took some pictures of Scott and the park people and they took one of Scott and me.

Often I flew with canoes tied to the tops of the Beaver's floats and would drop off canoe parties at the headwaters of the Nahanni, the Moose Ponds. Sometimes I would take them further downstream to a lake or along the banks of the Nahanni River.

The (Salvey) Dene Indians of this area call the falls Naili Cho, which translates to "Big Water Falling Down." Nahanni means "People over there — far away." The word was used by the eighteenth-century Athapaskan-speaking tribes who traveled and hunted in this area.

Larry's son, Scott, and Larry after landing about 300 yards upstream from Virginia Falls in 1973. The nearest road was about 140 miles.

About fifty-three miles upstream from the falls, the Rabbit Kettle River enters the Nahanni near the park's western boundary. A short distance south is Rabbit Kettle Hotsprings. This awesome and beautiful terraced mound of calcium carbonate was the destination of many canoe and raft parties I flew in. From there, they would canoe and raft down river to Nahanni Butte, where I would pick them up and fly back to Watson Lake.

The Moose Ponds are 100 miles northwest of the Park boundary. Over the course of the first 100 miles, known as the Rock Gardens, the river drops some 2,000 feet in the form of continuous Class II and Class III white waters.

I remember one flight with the Beaver in the early 1970s. I dropped off two young men from Norway at the Moose Ponds. They later told me that they put holes in the bottom of their canoe. When they were short of food they came upon a moose which had been killed by wolves. The moose was still warm and provided them with a welcome feast.

Below the falls, the river enters Fourth Canyon. As we flew the canyon, we were buffeted with moderate turbulence. Below, where the Flat River joins the Nahanni, Third Canyon begins and the Nahanni River suddenly makes a 90° turn at "The Gate." Janey took several pictures of this site between the high, narrow vertical cliffs.

Second Canyon cuts through the Funeral Range and the marks on my sectional chart show where I once flew into Deadmen Valley many years ago.

This old sectional chart of the Nahanni Country is held together with yellowed Scotch tape and is taped to a sectional chart of Watson Lake. Beyond Second Canyon, a few miles ahead, the map shows a series of black dots at the junction where Prairie Creek comes in from the north and flows into the Nahanni River.

As a boy growing up in Spokane, Washington, I read an article called "Headless Valley." It is the story about the McLeod brothers. Willie McLeod set off in 1905 for a gold prospecting trip to the South Nahanni River, taking his brother Frank and an engineer. On a previous trip, Willie had lost a large amount of gold when his canoe tipped over and he had managed to save only a few ounces.

The party disappeared up the Nahanni and after a year, Charlie McLeod started a search for his brothers. He found their bones in a camp where Prairie Creek enters the South Nahanni River. It looked as if one brother was trying to reach a gun and the other was killed in his bed. According to the story, the murderer took the gold and was never found. The article went on to say the Indians avoided that place and that the wind blowing down the valley made an unearthly sound.

At a later date, Charlie's son said that the bodies of his uncles were without their heads. Whatever happened, the valley is marked on my sectional map as Deadmen Valley and is also known as Headless Valley. Looking at my sectional chart, I notice that it's distinctly marked with black dots, giving it a dark appearance on the map.

The air was a bit rough and the bare mountain peaks of the Mackenzies loomed threateningly above our tiny ship on both sides of the canyon walls.

About 8:30 p.m., we entered Deadmen Valley, where Prairie Creek enters the Nahanni from the north. It looked somewhat the way I remembered it from the early 1970s. The red-roofed cabin where our firefighting camp was located was on the south side of the river, much as I recalled when I stayed there in a tent. There was a makeshift pole dock down a steep bank below the cabin, where I would load and unload the Red Beaver when I flew men and freight in from Nahanni Butte, Fort Simpson, and Fort Liard to Deadmen Valley. A helicopter would fly the men from this camp to nearby fires that threatened to burn up the proposed Nahanni National Park. They wanted to put them out as quickly as possible so they wouldn't leave an ugly scar.

A DC-3 would land at the village of Nahanni Butte on a gravel strip and

Larry in his favorite airplane, the Red Beaver, taking off of the South Nahanni River in Deadmen Valley to pick up another load of freight.

I would freight the supplies up to the camp in the red float-equipped Beaver, CF-IBP. One day, a beautiful, young woman stepped out of the DC-3 and I asked her if she would like to fly into Deadmen Valley.

"Yes, I would like to do a story and take photographs of the place. I'm a freelance writer and photographer from France. My name is Sheila."

"Hi, my name is Larry. You're welcome to fly into camp."

Sheila spent three days in camp at Deadmen Valley. One day, we flew down to Kraus' cabin, located at the hot springs at the east end of First Canyon.

Sheila took a photo of me taking a picture as we flew low into First Canyon at the east end of Deadmen Valley. She also took a great photo of the Red Beaver as I flew off the river in front of the camp. Happy memories of that time live on.

Once, while flying in this Nahanni Country, I met a Mr. Turner and landed a float plane at his home. He wrote several books about his life as a bush pilot in the Nahanni country.

After flying by the red-roofed forestry cabin, I pointed to a ridge up the mountain side a mile south of the entrance to First Canyon and said, "That's the ridge I flew over when I disappeared into the clouds and thought I was going to die for sure. I remember uttering two words "Oh God."

Just after I related the story, we entered First Canyon and a force gripped our ship and shook us violently. It was different than normal turbulence, which hits, releases, and then hits again. This force didn't let go! I could feel

Larry is taking a picture of First Canyon while flying the Red Beaver. The ridge on the right hand side is where Larry's plane disappeared in the clouds and Larry said he through he had "bought the farm."

it in the controls and didn't know if I would live to see another day.

The canyon walls were narrow and steep and we were down quite close to the river when we entered. I knew there was no point in trying to climb out, as we would probably be through First Canyon before I could climb high enough to clear the peaks of the mighty Mackenzie Mountains. I also knew it could be even worse near the mountain tops. As I gripped the control wheel tightly, not knowing what fate would bring, a feeling of impending doom prevailed. I felt that death on the canyon walls, so close to our wing tips, was indeed a possibility. Once again apprehension filled my cockpit world, much as it had in 1971 when I flew the Red Beaver into thick clouds above that nearby ridge just south of here.

Flying on the ragged edge was an incredible high and all my senses were on full alert as we banked through the narrow, twisting canyon. My adrenalin was in full swing as this very scared pilot finally saw the end of the canyon and knew that there were only a few more bends to negotiate before we got to the wide valley beyond. There, the Nahanni enters the Liard and the country becomes fairly flat. I said to myself, "If fate allows us safe passage through, I never plan to fly through here again!" After I maneuvered carefully around the remaining bends, the force gripping our faithful ship suddenly spit us out the east end of the canyon into smooth, calm air.

My hands were cold and wet, my knuckles white from gripping the controls hard, and my body was fatigued from the flight through the Nahanni country, but I was one happy pilot and glad to be around to fly another day. Once again, the ominous spirits of Deadmen Valley had made me look death in the eye, in the form of vertical rock canyon walls just off the wing tips.

I had planned to look at Kraus's cabin and the hot springs behind it, located at the east end of First Canyon, but forgot all about it until a day or so later.

Life now had a quality and sweetness to it that I would never have known if I hadn't flown through First Canyon that day, not knowing what fate would decide.

About twenty-eight miles downstream, the Indian village of Nahanni Butte came into view. We were going to overnight there in a tent, but decided to fly on to Fort Liard and spend the night there. It was at this village of Nahanni Butte that an Indian woman made me a beautiful pair of moccasins from moose hide. Beautiful, intricate beadwork of her own design covered the mink-lined tops of these special moccasins. I have pleasant memories of this village from times past.

About 12,000 years ago, at the end of the last ice age, the earliest inhabitants of the Nahanni region migrated across the Bering land bridge from Asia. Ancestors of the Slavey Indians, who live in the Nahanni area, moved into this area about 5,000 years ago.

The fur traders were the Indian's first contact with Europeans. The Indians traded for guns, knives, and later tents and portable stoves that relieved some of the hardships of living on the land. But in many ways, they still retain their old way of life.

When I was in that firefighting camp at Deadmen Valley in 1971, I remember my first impression. When I exited the Beaver on the pole dock, I noticed strips of moose meat drying on a line in the sun near the bank of the river. The only Indian who spoke English to me was the foreman; the rest spoke their own language. They minded their own business and blended in with the wilderness way of life.

The Nahanni country has moose, woodland caribou, dall sheep, mule and whitetail deer, and beaver. Grizzly are not common, but black bear are often seen. The area has good fishing for grayling, pike, dolly varden, lake trout, pickerel, and whitefish. Forests of aspen, white spruce, and balsam cover the valleys. It is a beautiful place.

CHAPTER 11

Fort Liard Northwest Territories

From Nahanni Butte, we flew south toward Fort Liard, some fifty-three air miles away. It was getting dark and we looked forward to landing, stretching our legs, getting some food, and having a good night's sleep. Due to forest fires in the area, the visibility was poor, especially looking east toward Fort Simpson. It was a little better to the south in the direction of Fort Liard and much better to the west.

About twenty miles south of Nahanni Butte, there is now a gravel highway that begins a few miles north of Fort Nelson, off the Alaska Highway, and goes north through Fort Liard and on to Yellowknife. This area was roadless when I flew here in the 1970s and Fort Liard could only be reached by river boat, airplane, or trail.

Fatigue had set in and the flight to Fort Liard, Northwest Territories, seemed to be a lot farther than it was, but the air was smooth and the broad, winding Liard River was beautiful and soothing.

Fort Liard is eighteen miles north of the British Columbia border and twenty-two miles east of the Yukon border. The airport is 701 feet above sea level and the gravel runway is 3,000 feet long.

North of the airport about ten miles I reported my position on 122.1, the frequency used to advise local air traffic. There is no Flight Service Station and flight plans are opened and closed with Fort Simpson, Northwest Territories, by phone. I couldn't reach them by radio. Fort Liard is on the east side of the Liard River. A pilot in another airplane behind me asked if he could land first, as he was having a problem. I consented, and we flew to

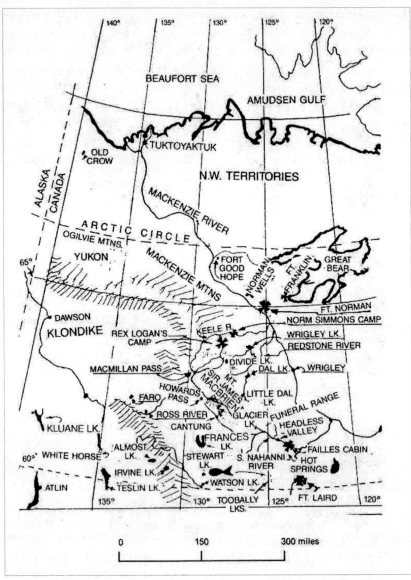

This map shows the southern part of the Yukon and Northwest Territories.

the southwest, circled around and landed behind a tail dragger Scout.

Steve Malesko, the Scout's pilot, told me that his problem was a damaged prop, which was making his engine vibrate badly, which was the reason he needed to land as quickly as possible. It had happened when his plane had nosed over after he landed on a mountainside in the Nahanni country and turned around to take off downhill. He had been scouting out a place to hunt this fall when the accident occurred.

We touched down just before dark, tied down the airplane and got a lift with a pilot-engineer who worked for a local flying service at the airfield. He drove us to the hotel and we obtained a room. We were able to get a man to open the store below our room and we bought fruit, soup, and milk. The room had a refrigerator and stove and we were hungry. I felt like a starved pilot after that wild ride through the Nahanni country.

Later, I spent time going over aviation maps for the following day. We planned to fly to Dease Lake and then on to Atlin Lake, both in British Columbia. I hadn't been back to Atlin since I flew as a bush pilot out of Watson Lake in the 1970s and I remembered it was a beautiful place. We called flights into Atlin "the booze run" because liquor was cheaper in British Columbia than in the Yukon, so we had a steady order to purchase booze at Atlin and fly it back to Watson Lake.

Around 2400, I finally fell asleep, exhausted, but happy to be alive after the white-knuckle flight through First Canyon. Life was sweet.

Sunday, Aug. 1, 1993

A green canoe drifts by on the Liard River; it's empty and going solo down this mighty river. I'm sitting on a bank overlooking the swift brown-green waters of the river, at the Indian village of Fort Liard.

When I was working a fire in Deadmen Valley in 1971, flying the Red Beaver, I overnighted here a few times. I met the most beautiful young Indian woman that I had ever seen. She was taking care of the Indian children who boarded at Fort Liard during the winter months. The parents would bring them here from their hunting and trapping camps, and the children would attend school for the winter months. Machelle would bring the children down to the river and watch me take off in the Beaver.

I'm sitting under poplar trees and a bee is buzzing around my cup. It feels good to be alone. I like alone. The leaves of the poplar tree are waving and flapping with a dry sound. A nice breeze makes me feel good--just right.

Flying over the Nahanni yesterday was awesome, with the towering, forbidding Mackenzie Mountains enclosed around my ship as we flew deep into the Valley of the Nahanni. We flew low over two moose in a small lake.

As we flew into First Canyon, I soon realized that I was an insignificant intruder. The turbulence shook my ship rather severely as we flew through the narrow canyon rock walls. I felt that if I could just make it through the last few turns and out of First Canyon to the wide valley where the Nahanni flows into the Liard, I'd be so happy. I felt that if I could pull this one out I'd be on a real high and have a memory to relive. I'd be so happy to be alive. A chipmunk talks to me from about six feet away, maybe looking for a snack.

1005: An Otter on floats, blue and white, with a red canoe strapped to its side, just flew by and is still climbing upstream. It sounds like the engine is laboring and very tired, as it slowly climbs away from the river.

1009: The Otter is flying back, north to the Nahanni River to drop off the canoe party. It is still struggling as it slowly climbs.

Albert Faille, a prospector, came to the South Nahanni in 1927. He was an expert river man and prospected for gold in the Nahanni country for nearly forty years, well into his seventies. Just above Virginia Falls is a boat he built after carrying the lumber on his back from the bottom to the top of the falls. A picture was taken of me in 1971, standing next to Faille's old boat at the top of the falls.

After walking back to the hotel, we walked to the river and Janey took pictures of log homes and the old deserted Hudson Bay Store that had been operating when I flew the Beaver here in 1971. We talked to people by the float dock who were going out in the bush. It was quiet and pleasant. We then walked to the nearby café to get coffee and a ride to the airport, but it

Janey took this picture shortly after we took off from Fort Liard on course to Dease Lake, B.C.

was closed. We inquired at a nearby information center and talked to a young

Indian woman. She didn't know when the café would open. The sign said 1000, but it was already past that time. Fort Liard was a quiet place on Sunday morning.

We caught a ride with a white man, who said he was the town manager, and he agreed to take us to the airport.

"How has the road affected the Indians at Fort Liard? When I was here in the 1970s, there were no roads."

"It's made them much more dependent on the government."

The airport was quiet and no one was around when we arrived. I walked to the gas pump and into a nearby hangar owned by a local flying service, but no one was there. The office inside the hangar was open and I used a phone.

Steve Malesko, the pilot of the Scout whom we met the previous day, arrived and drove us around town looking for someone to gas us up. We couldn't find anyone, so Steve turned on the pump. I topped the tanks and paid him what he thought the fuel price was.

"Steve, what do you do for a living?"

"I'm involved with several ventures with a partner, but I can't lift much because I have a bad back. I flew into the mountains (Nahanni country) in a helicopter with my wife, another man and the pilot who was a good friend of mine. We flew into a cloud and crashed into a mountainside. My wife, the pilot and the other man died. I was seriously injured and have had a bad back since then. A lot of people have died in the Nahanni area."

"Yes, I know! One of the pilots that I flew with out of Watson Lake, Dennis Ball, was killed with another man while flying an Otter during bad weather up Lafferty Creek, located a few miles north of Deadmen Valley. We had a scary flight through First Canyon yesterday and I was almost killed in bad weather in 1971, when I disappeared into the clouds by Deadmen Valley."

CHAPTER 12

Flying Across British Columbia

I thanked Steve for his help and autographed a copy of my book for him. We said goodbye, I cranked up our ship and taxied to the runway.

1215: *Off Fort Liard on course to Dease Lake.*

1240: *Left the Northwest Territories behind and entered British Columbia.*

1245: *6,750 feet, heading 210°. It's a beautiful day over British Columbia. Filed flight plan by phone with Fort Simpson.*

1252: *Flew near Scatter River Airstrip.*

I flew the Watson Lake Flying Service's twin-engine Piper Aztec CF-HIA into the Scatter River strip many times for Dempsey Callison, an outfitter who guided in this area. Dempsey was a handsome young Indian man with a lot of good-looking women as his admirers. When I would fly new hunters and supplies into Dempsey's camp every ten or fifteen days, there would often be a new good-looking woman going along to cook or help Dempsey in some way. He met these women during the winter months when he was in Southern British Columbia. Later Dempsey became a minister, I was told, and changed his ways.

East of the Scatter River Country are three World War II bombers,

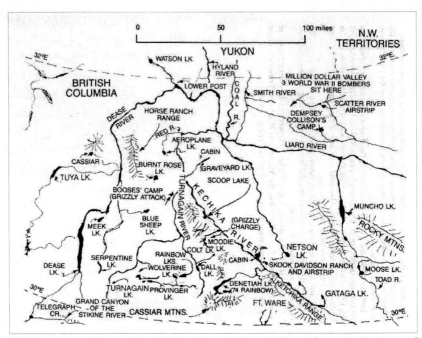

This is a map of the northern Rocky Mountains and shows the route Janey and Larry flew to Dease Lake.

which landed in a valley just east of the old Smith River Airport by mistake in a snowstorm. It's called the Million Dollar Valley and the bombers were still visible when I flew over them on the flight to Scatter River.

We had an early winter in the fall of 1974, that I remember well. I wrote in my journal on October 5, 1974, that the weather the past ten days had turned to snow and cold in the higher elevations. I tried unsuccessfully to get into Plateau Lake, and those hunters were picked up later by a helicopter. This lake was thinly frozen, so I was unable to land there. I flew skis into the Scatter River airstrip, twenty miles distant. I was also able to fly into a small lake using floats on IBP to pick up some German hunters, as a small bay was unfrozen. I told them to leave all their belongings, including toothbrushes. My Red Beaver IBP performed superbly and we were off the water and into the air before reaching the ice.

One of the Germans, himself a pilot, pounded my back and said "Good, good!" It had been four months exactly since I had made the last trip on skis--a short summer.

There were constant reminders that we really were "braving the untamed wilderness." That fall a hunter I had flown in earlier to a hunting camp got lost and was never found. He went ahead of the guide on the trail and said he could find his own way back. Another man, a prospector, was also lost and never found. A pilot dropped him off at Divide Lake, and two months later I flew in the Royal Canadian Mounted Police. We flew low, but no trace was found and fresh snow and ice on the lake prevented our landing. We found his neatly set-up camp, but no prospector. The scene was stark and etched deeply in my mind as we recognized the tragic end to this man's dream.

In 1983 his thick glasses, some tattered clothing and his wristwatch were found near Divide Lake. Darell Nelson, who still owns Northwest Territory Outfitters and guides in that area, said the watch began ticking. He thought that a grizzly bear might have killed the prospector, but no one will ever know for sure. A guide and a camp helper from two separate camps also lost their lives in accidents that fall.

That was a season of tough flying for me and I felt very fortunate that I experienced no accidents and still had my hide.

1320: *Just passed over Fishing Lake--right on course.*

We flew over the Liard River about a few miles east of the Liard River Airstrip. As we looked south down the Alaska Highway, Muncho Lake was clearly visible.

We flew over the Kechika River, about eight miles south of Scoop Lake. Many memories of this familiar place surfaced. My first flight to Scoop Lake was in 1969. I was flying a Beaver for B.C. Yukon Air Service with freight for the outfitter Frank Cook, who was located in his main camp at Moodie Lake.

It was August 10, 1969, and that was my first trip to this area, so I had my sectional maps on my lap. This was one of my first flights for B.C. Yukon Air Service. The weather was lousy after take-off and I had to climb over the cloud cover, but I could see holes through the layers. I was flying, feeling good and following a river when I noticed that, according to my map, the river was running the wrong direction. I discovered I was not sure of my location. In other words, I was lost!

A short time later, I saw a lake through a hole in the clouds and thought

I spotted some pack dogs by a cabin. This made me feel better, since I could land and ask directions. Upon landing, I taxied the Beaver to shore, tied up, and proceeded to climb up the bank, intending to walk to the cabin. As I topped the bank, I met a large mass of fur coming toward me about fifteen feet away. I froze! The grizzly didn't like my looks any better than I liked his. I walked slowly backward to the plane and, much to my relief, the grizzly went the other direction. Looking at my map, I decided I was probably at Scoop Lake and Moodie Lake was about fifteen miles southwest.

I flew on to Moodie Lake and met Frank Cooke for the first time. Frank, a lean six-footer who looked like a cowboy, had wrangled horses since his childhood. He was a nice-looking, intelligent individual, friendly, well-organized, and seemed completely in charge of every situation. I explained my encounter with the bear and asked, "Frank, are there any pack dogs by the cabin?"

He replied, "No, but I'll bet they were bears, and they probably wrecked my cabin." Frank rounded up a hunter, and we flew back to Scoop Lake to deal with the grizzlies.

Frank describes this event: "I remember it like it was yesterday, and it was the first time we met. You flew in and asked me if there were big dogs or some other animals down at Scoop Lake, and I said there shouldn't be, and no people either. Having lived in the north for so long, I thought there had to be a bear fooling around. I also knew in my mind that they would smash a window and get in my cookhouse and wreck everything, which is exactly what they did. I asked the hunter if he wanted to have some fun, and he said, 'Doing what?' When I explained it to him, he became excited and asked, 'How can we get down there?' I told him I would hire you to fly us down to Scoop Lake to take a look, and then we would fly back to Moodie Lake. So I chartered the Beaver, and away we went."

Frank continued, "When we tied up at Scoop Lake, I remember looking out the window of the Beaver, and sure enough, there was one grizzly in the yard. I wasn't going to let the hunter shoot him, but I looked over at the cookhouse door and saw that it was open and all the windows were knocked out and knew there would be a mess in the cabin. The bear started to run, and I said, 'Shoot him!' He did and killed him. The gun had no sooner gone off when out the door came another grizzly, and then out the window another. I hated to shoot them, but I knew I had to, as they would never leave and are very destructive. One started down the lake, but the other one started toward us at the lakeshore by the plane."

"I said to the hunter, 'You take the one going down the lake, and I'll take the one heading for us,' as he was close, and I wasn't sure how good he could shoot. I don't like being too close to a grizzly with a strange hunter in case he wounds him. Grizzlies can be very dangerous at close quarters. I knew my gun and knew I could kill the bear with one shot, and I did. He shot and, sure enough! He only wounded his bear. I walked over to the dead one and then finished off the one he had wounded. I can't remember the hunter's name, but he sure was excited. He had never seen or participated in that kind of event. It was just another day to me. I have seen lots of these really dangerous situations in my life."

I sat down on one of the bunks to write out a flight ticket. My pants suddenly became very damp, and a strong odor penetrated the air. The bears had urinated on the mattress, and, confined in the warm cockpit of the Beaver, I had to endure this odor all the way back to Watson Lake.

I was supposed to fly over Scoop Lake but was south of my course; however, it worked out perfectly because we were now going to fly over Moodie Lake. The last time I flew in this country was in 1975, for Watson Lake Flying Service. Scott and I overnighted by Scoop Lake in a tent one night. Thick smoke covered the wilderness as it was a very bad fire season that summer. I told Scott to remember the sunset, the cabin, and this unique time in our lives. The next morning we flew to nearby Colt Lake, which is a small body of water created by a beaver dam. We flew groceries and freight to a sheep hunting camp of Frank Cooke's.

A few miles southeast of Colt Lake by the Kechika River is Skook Davidson's old ranch, just below Terminus Mountain, 120 miles south and a bit east of Watson Lake. His name was John Oglivie Davidson. Skook was a nickname given to him by the Indians. It comes from the Indian word Skookum, meaning "strong," which he lived up to. He was born in Longside, Scotland in 1882 and came to Canada when he was fifteen years old. Skook came to live in the Kechika Valley in the northern end of the Rocky Mountain Trench and established his Diamond J Ranch at the foot of Terminus Mountain in 1939. He remained there until 1972, when ill health forced him to go to the Whitehorse Hospital and then to a private hospital in Vancouver, British Columbia, where he died. I remember Skook calling in on the radio, usually every day, when I flew for Watson Lake Flying Service.

Frank Cooke told me this information about Skook. Frank lived with

Janey and Larry are flying toward Moodie Lakes. Outfitter Frank Cooke had his main camp at the first lake, where the five grizzly bears charged.

Skook for many years when he was a young man. Skook worked on all the big cattle ranches in the Caribou Country and packed mules for Old Cataline all through the Caribou gold rushes. He was a packer and freighter throughout the north. He went through World War I and was decorated for bravery. He was a special policeman for the north while I was with him. He loved his horses and treated them like his own children. He never married or had any children. Skook drank rum with Winston Churchill and knew him personally. He also went for a flight with Billy Bishop over France during the first war.

I flew freight for Skook in the Beaver and landed on the Kechika River one day. Skook met me with a horse-drawn wagon on the east bank of the river. He was about ninety years old then and didn't say much. He sat up straight and looked to be a hardy individual. I unloaded the Beaver and put the freight in the wagon. I believe Skook had arthritis. It was a privilege to see him in the wilderness that he loved and knew so well.

As we approached Moodie Lakes, Janey started taking videos while I talked about Frank's camp below and some of the memories I had of this special place. There are three lakes Frank's old camp was on the first lake. I remember all the great meals I ate there and the good times we all had at this camp. It was exciting, full of adventure, during those wonderful bush pilot days, flying in that vast northern wilderness. One evening, five grizzly bears

Big game outfitter Frank Cooke, his wife, Hatti, his son, Terry, and Larry at Cooke's main hunting camp at Moodie Lake.

charged through camp, and the one that Frank shot dropped about two feet from his foot.

After flying over Moodie Lake, we flew west over another valley and could see Dall Lake to the south. Southeast a few miles from Dall Lake is Denetiah Lake, where four of us once caught a lot of rainbow trout in a stream that flows into that lake. We caught seventy-four trout and kept thirty-two that were between two and nine pounds. That was the best fishing I've ever had.

We flew over the Dall River and picked up the Turnagain River, on which I have landed. It looks like a snake and is aptly named. I remember a special flight over the Turnagain River in the early 1970s when I flew for Watson Lake Flying Service. Early morning flights were a special treat, so often I was one of the first pilots on the lake and in the air. My destination was a flight to a mining camp on Provinger Lake, a few miles south of the Turnagain River. After my preflight check I pointed my craft down the lake, full power, and we were airborne within seconds in the thick, cool air.

The light before sunrise had a special quality. The valleys were still dark and formless, with only a faint light to the east over the Rocky Mountains. As I slipped smoothly through the clear air, a special early

In spring of 1970, a forestry worker, Forest Ranger Dave of Lower Post B.C., and Larry caught 74 Rainbow at Denetiah Lake, B.C., and kept 32 of them between 2 and 9 pounds. Larry flew in B.C. Yukon Air Service's Cessna 185.

morning feeling of being the only one in this visible sky, of peace and of oneness with God and His creation came over me. The steady drone of the engine, with wings attached to my back, made my world secure. Soaring like an eagle, looking down upon this untouched wilderness, gave me a feeling unlike anything else in life. Peaceful, alive, my world was here. It was perfect at this moment.

The advancing dawn brightened the sky, and the valley became alive. Trees, flowing rivers, and meadows revealed themselves and the world below took form. Flying near the Turnagain River at eight thousand feet, I began playing a game with the pure white cumulus tops, soaring in and around the valleys and peaks of these early morning giants of the sky. The air was still smooth as we danced with the clouds.

My favorite poem was written by John Magee, an American pilot in the RCAF during World War II, shortly before he lost his life in an air battle. It describes something close to what I felt as I soared in and around these white mountains of clouds. This sonnet is titled, "High Flight," and has become the official poem of the U.S. Air Force.

High Flight

Oh, I have slipped the surly bonds of earth
And danced the skies on laughter-silvered wings;
Sunward I've climbed, and joined the tumbling mirth
Of sun-split clouds and done a hundred things
You have not dreamed of wheeled and soared and swung
High in the sunlit silence. Hovering there
I've chased the shouting wind along, and flung
My eager craft through footless halls of air.
Up, up the long, delirious, burning blue
I've topped the windswept heights with easy grace
Where never lark, or even eagle flew
And, while with silent, lifting mind I've trod
The high untrespassed sanctity of space,
Put out my hand, and touched the face of God.

In later years I often relived this most special time when I soared my craft in and around the high mountains of white clouds. The Cassiar Mountains are so familiar, yet it's as if I've been in a deep sleep it is both a long-ago and a familiar scene. Time and distance change, as in a dream world.

1434: *Flew over Eagle Lake a few minutes ago. I flew for the outfitter, George Dalziel, into this area in the early seventies. Dease Lake is up ahead.*

The airport is a speck up ahead and beautiful Dease Lake is off to the right. It will be nice to stop, stretch, maybe have coffee and a bite to eat. We are heading straight in for runway 02. The elevation at the airport is 2,600 feet and the paved runway is 6,000 feet long.

After touchdown, we taxied to the east end of the airport and up a hill to Pacific Western Helicopter Base, where I could see a gas pump.

After leaning the mixture to kill the engine, I stepped outside and noticed a woman coming out of the log building nearby, on the other side of a helicopter hangar.

"Hi, my name is Larry, could we get some fuel?"

Jack O'Conner, the outdoor editor of *Outdoor Life Magazine,* Larry Whitesitt and a hunter are posing at Frank Cooke and Sons hunting camp at Colt Lake in B.C. Larry flew Jack in and picked him up after he bagged a good-sized stone sheep. This was Jack's last sheep hunt. Larry and Jack corresponded after the hunt.

"Sure, my name is Sharon Reed."

We walked to the log building where we were offered fresh-baked cake and coffee.

Sharon and her husband, Jim, operate this base. Jim flies the helicopter and Sharon operates the radio and runs the office. Sharon offered the car at the base so we could go to a nearby store to get some film. We drove to the store, but they didn't have the film we needed and instead we bought fruit and pop.

When we returned to the base, Jim had returned and we met. I left them a book and thanked them for their warm hospitality. Sharon and Jim are from New Zealand, but they wanted to see Canada and planned on retiring in New Zealand.

Off at 1640: *On course to Atlin Lake. I called Whitehorse radio on 126.7 and told them I estimated Atlin in one hour and twenty minutes, at about 1800.*

1652: *6,500 feet and mostly clear. On a heading of 270°. Tachita Lake and Granite Lake ahead.*

1724: *By Prairie and Gun lakes, north twenty miles is Kedahda Lake.*

1728: *Over Disella Lake. I can see the glacier's path that went through here in a northwest direction and left numerous lakes.*

1733: *Nakina Lake can be seen to the south as we fly over Nakina River.*

This land between Dease Lake and Atlin is mostly wilderness. Surprise Lake is off our starboard wing and according to the map, Atlin Lake and the town of Atlin should be just around the bend of a small mountain, a few miles ahead.

CHAPTER 13

Atlin, Gem of the North

Atlin Lake's beautiful deep blue waters sparkled in the late afternoon sun, to the west, as we flew around a mountain on the south side of Pine Creek. The last time I flew to Atlin was in 1975. I remembered it was a pretty place, but now it seemed to be the most beautiful place that I had ever seen. Majestic glacier-covered mountains lined the western shores of this great lake.

Atlin Lake is seventy miles long and two to five miles wide. It is the largest natural lake in British Columbia and the northern end extends into the Yukon Territory. This lake is the source of the mighty Yukon River; you can boat from Atlin Lake to Whitehorse through a series of lakes and waterways, and from Whitehorse north to Dawson City and then west through Alaska to the Bering Sea.

As we descended, I was struck with the raw beauty of this lake and the surrounding glacier-covered mountains. Peterson Field, the Atlin airport, is located a few miles east of the quaint town. The airport's elevation is 2,348 feet and the gravel strip is 3,950 feet long. I called on the Air Traffic Frequency of 123.2 to let local traffic know that I would be landing on runway 18. We touched down at 1806 and taxied off the runway to the empty terminal building, on the west side of the airport, where there is a phone. I called Whitehorse and closed my flight plan. After tying down the airplane to some rocks, we had a chance to stretch and get our earth legs working.

Lorie O'Neill and Janey Youngblood are standing in front of Lorie's Fireweed
Bed & Breakfast Inn in Atlin, B.C., in August 1993.

Sunday, August 1, 1993

1820: *Sitting on a table bench at the Peterson Airport, Atlin, British
Columbia.*

This airport is named after Herman Peterson, a bush pilot who lives in
Atlin. For many years Herman owned and operated Coast Range Airways,
Ltd., here at Atlin, with Beavers and Otters as well as a helicopter. He is a
soft-spoken bush pilot and a living legend of the north. I first met Herman in
the early 1970s when he landed at Watson Lake Airport in his Luscomb.

Friendly, congenial Jamie Tait, who owns Summit Air Flying Service
gave us a lift to town. We asked if he could tell us of a good place to stay,
and he recommended the Fireweed Inn Bed and Breakfast.

As we drove into the town of Atlin, we were awed by the beauty of the
lake, the nearby mountains and the quaint town, which has a year-round
population of some 400 people   Atlin is built on the side of a hill, on the east
side of Atlin Lake.

Jamie stopped at a quaint, blue two-story home and stepped inside. An
attractive, friendly woman named Lorrie O'Neill, who owns and runs the inn,
met us by the door and showed us to our room on the second story.

1928: *I'm sitting on a double bed at the Fireweed Inn, a unique bed and breakfast establishment here at the beautiful town site of Atlin, British Columbia. The glaciers across the blue waters of this huge lake are even lovelier than I remember.*

This is truly a place of peace, of rest and I'm so happy and pleased to be here. It's so quiet. I'm lying on my bed looking at a glacier. Later, we walked down the hill to the beach and out on a dock. Across the lake is Atlin Mountain.

2110: *Sitting on a dock at Atlin Lake in front of a log cabin. Seagulls cry, a gorgeous view, pleasant wind and wonderful air.*

2139: *Sitting in an open area at the Atlin Inn, the only place we could get something to eat, and we've ordered pizza.*

2147: *A Cessna 185 float plane just landed on the lake and is tying up to a nearby dock. A Beaver float plane also sits tied to a dock. Looking across Atlin Lake to an island with three sailboats and one catamaran anchored and protected from the prevailing westerly wind by the island. I sketch the scene in my green notebook journal.*

2207: *A Beech 18 just passed over on final to the airport. A glacier can be seen on a mountain to the southwest, rising above the water. Jamie Tait has been flying this twin-engine Beech 18 of his to an airstrip at a mining camp south of Atlin, 100 miles away.*

After we finished the large, delicious pizza, we walked back to the Fireweed Inn. A hungry-looking dog followed us and we fed him some of our leftover pizza. After we returned to our room, I wrote in my journal.

2242: *Atlin is an Indian name that translates to "Big Water."*

Monday, August 2, 1993

0735: *At the kitchen table for breakfast and am having my first cup of coffee. It's good. Janey, the photographer, just came down. The sun's*

Janey and Larry are flying over Tagish Lake, which is connected to Atlin Lake and is part of the source of the Yukon River. They are heading toward Skagway, Alaska.

shining brightly through the window as pancakes and ham are being prepared.

After breakfast we walked to the Atlin Trading post in search of film. After we left the store, we walked up to Lyman Sands' service station and he gave us a ride to the airport. I taxied the plane to the gas pump and Lyman, who has the gas concession, turned on the pump. I topped both tanks. Lyman is also the Customs Officer and delivers water from the lake in a water truck to the houses in Atlin. Lorrie O'Neill has a large water tank in the basement of the Fireweed Inn that Lyman fills. Lyman Sands came to Atlin after he retired, but you would never know he's retired. His wife, Ann Sands, owns and runs a restaurant by their service station.

After fueling we taxied to runway 18 and departed for Kluane National Park to get pictures of the largest ice fields in the world outside the polar regions. The weather was sunny and the air smooth as we flew across Atlin Lake. After we crossed the lake, we cruised on a heading of 259° over Graham Inlet and Taku Arm, which are part of Tagish Lake.

We then flew by Racine and Shelly Lakes and over the Tatshi River just south of Tatshi Lake. Most of these lakes are a green-turquoise color, which

This picture was taken near the border of Alaska, close to the largest ice field in the world outside of the polar regions.

is caused by glacier silt.

> 1227: *At 8,075 feet, we passed south of Bennett Lake. Lindeman Lake is just south of Bennett Lake and the Yukon and White Pass narrow gauge railroad track follows the eastern shore of both of these lakes. Lindeman and Bennett lakes were on the route most of the gold-rushers took to Dawson City from 1897-1899.*

We proceeded northwest of Bennett Lake for fifty miles and got some terrific photos of glacier-covered mountains as far as we could see. Clouds began to cover the peaks and we were probably just inside the Yukon Territory, close to the eastern edge of Kluane Park when we made a 180° turn and headed for Skagway, Alaska. Those incredible ice fields extend for hundreds of miles to the southwest and northwest. That vast glacier wilderness, which we're privileged to see for the first time, was inspiring.

A phenomena all too well-known to bush pilots occurred. This was a rugged glacier-covered mountain wilderness where I could not see a landing field or safe place to set down, and the engine started to run rough. I felt the panel and said, "It's vibrating, the engine is running rough. Can't you feel it?" This phenomena takes place with even the smoothest, sweetest running engines whenever there's no safe place to land. You're sure the engine will

This is a picture of Kluane National Park and the beginning of the huge ice fields.

soon quit. Once you're over a safe area where you can land, the engine runs smoothly again.

This vast glacier wilderness was certainly beautiful, but I realized it would be a most dangerous place to land safely if the engine did indeed quit or the weather deteriorated.

Always when I fly, there is an underlying fear and respect that has accumulated over thirty-four years of flying for weather hazards, mechanical problems, pilot error and lastly, fate. I've had more than enough close calls to last my lifetime. I'm a fair weather pilot now and have nothing to prove to myself or anyone else. So many of the pilots I knew and flew with in the north were killed in flying accidents, mostly due to bad weather. There is a tremendous high when flying on the edge; however I don't feel I need that high any more and prefer smooth, good-weather flights.

We flew back, retracing our route on a heading of 179°. As we flew near Bennett Lake we turned right and went south above the narrow-gauge railroad tracks of the Yukon and White Pass Railroad toward Skagway. A few miles off our starboard wing, according to my sectional chart, is Chilkoot Pass.

What really surprised me about this country were the narrow valleys and steep glacier-covered mountains. I thought Lindeman and Bennett lakes were in a wide valley similar to the country around Atlin. I have a lot of respect for those adventurous gold-rushers who crossed Chilkoot Pass to Lindeman Lake. They must have been staggered by the rugged country and I'm sure they asked themselves more than once, "What am I doing here and how will I survive this wilderness?"

Going south, we flew over Bernard and Summit lakes. The Skagway River begins at the south end of Summit Lake and descends to Taiya Inlet beside the town of Skagway. White Pass slipped beneath our wings.

Beyond a gap, I could see another glacier-covered mountain range and the air below the peaks had a bluish tint to it, like you find near the ocean or a large lake. Some stratus clouds just above us touched the patchy snow-covered mountain to our right. There, as we rounded a bend a minute later, the Pacific Ocean's Taiya Inlet appeared. Skagway could just barely be seen.

CHAPTER 14

Skagway, Gate to the Yukon

W hen I left Atlin, a flight plan was filed with Whitehorse radio to the Kluane National Park area and then to Skagway where I would close it. Because of the weather, we didn't fly as far northwest as we hoped to, so my estimated time of arrival in Skagway was shorter. I called the Flight Service Station at Juneau and gave them my new estimated time of arrival. There is no tower or Flight Service Station in Skagway, but I called on a frequency that the local pilots use to advise any traffic of their position. At that time, mine was about ten miles north, and I notified others that I was on a straight-in approach for runway 20, which favored the prevailing wind that Juneau Radio had given me. We landed on the paved 3,000 foot runway and turned left off the runway to a parking area.

1248: *Down at Skagway and the weather is sunny and warm.*

1343: *Parked behind dozens of Piper Cherokee airplanes. Good to be here!*

The following information was written by a Hearst newspaper in San Francisco after a ton of gold from the Klondike was unloaded from a ship there:

Skagway, Gate to the Yukon

Janey Youngblood standing next to Larry's airplane at the Skagway Airport
shortly after touchdown in August 1993.

*Gold! Gold in the Klondike! Thus began that great historic adventure
in the Yukon and Alaska that captured the vivid imagination of people
around the world. When George Washington Carmack and two Indian
companions, Skookum Jim and Tagish Charlie, found gold in a tributary
of the Klondike River in Canada's Yukon Territory in August 1896, they
had no idea that they would set off one of the greatest gold rushes in
history. Most of the good claims were already staked by the time the
rush really got moving in the summer of 1897, but this didn't stop
thousands of hopeful gold-seekers from boarding ships at Pacific ports
such as Seattle.*

*During the summer and autumn of 1897 and into that winter,
stampeders poured into the newly created Alaska tent and shack towns
of Skagway and Dyea the jumping-off points for the long, some 600-mile
journey to the goldfields. William Moore, a steamboat captain, founded
Skagway, located at the head of the White Pass Trail, and the town
quickly grew to 10,000 transient residents struggling to get their year's
worth of gear and supplies over the Coast Range and down to the Yukon
River's headwaters of Lindeman and Bennett lakes. Some nine miles to
the northwest, Dyea on the delta at the head of Taiya Inlet endured a
similar boomtown growth. Here gold-seekers poured ashore to pick
their way to the Chilkoot Trail into Canada.*

The greatest hardships the stampeders faced were on the Chilkoot Trail out of Dyea and the White Pass out of Skagway. Murders, suicides, disease, malnutrition and death from hypothermia, avalanche, and some said heartbreak, were faced on these tough trails. The Chilkoot was the toughest on men because pack animals could not be used on the steep slopes leading to Chilkoot Pass and until tramways were built in late 1897 and early 1898, the gold-rushers had to carry everything on their backs, or if they could afford it they could hire some of the local Indians to help them. The White Pass Trail was the animal-killer, as anxious prospectors overloaded and beat their pack animals and forced them over the rock terrain until they dropped. Over 3,000 animals died on this trail, many at the place called Dead Horse Gulch.

In the summer of 1898, Jack London and three partners debarked off the steamship Umatilla at Dyea and hauled their food and supplies on their backs to the Chilkoot Pass in about two and a half days; and then carried their gear another twenty-two miles to Lindeman Lake where they proceeded to build a boat. After felling the trees and sawing planks for the Yukon Belle, a carpenter and another partner in the group, using Jack's sketch of the flat-bottomed boat, built the Yukon Belle while Jack sewed the sails.

They successfully reached an old camp on Upper Island at Henderson Creek on October 9, 1898. They built a cabin, but only found fool's gold. The assayer said with a grin, "That's mica." Jack London didn't find a pot of gold in the Yukon, but he certainly found the pot of gold in the many tales he told about the Yukon. That first year, an estimated 20,000 to 30,000 spent an average of three months packing their outfits up the Chilkoot and White Pass Trails to Lindeman and Bennett Lakes where they built or bought boats to float the remaining 560 miles or so downriver to Dawson City and the Klondike, where an almost limitless supply of gold nuggets was said to be lying on the ground just waiting for the adventurers to bend over and pick up!

The distance from Dyea and Skagway to the lakes was only about 33 miles but each man trudged hundreds of miles back and forth along the trails, moving gear from cache to cache. By the middle of the summer of 1898, there were about 18,000 people at Dawson, with over 5,000 working the diggings. By August, many of the gold-seekers had started for home. Most were broke. The following year, there was an even larger exodus of miners when gold was discovered at Nome, Alaska. The great Klondike gold rush ended as suddenly as it had begun and towns like Dawson City and Skagway began to decline. Dyea and others disappeared, leaving only memories of what many considered the 19th century's last great adventure.

After flying in from the north to Skagway by Lindeman and Bennett Lakes, and flying near the Chilkoot and White Pass Trails, I have a new respect and understanding of the awesome challenge the gold-seekers faced. The country is very rugged with narrow trails, and is surrounded by high glacier-covered mountains. It must have taken true grit for them to carry on their backs a thousand pounds of supplies thirty-three miles to the lakes, where they still had to construct boats out of trees they cut down and sawed by hand into boards. The gold-rushers then had to face treacherous white water rapids near Marsh Lake and on the Yukon River. Many lost their boats and some their lives on the Yukon River.

I hope I'll be able to return to Skagway and hike the Chilkoot Trail to get a feel for the country on foot, and an appreciation of some of the hardships the gold seekers encountered as they hauled food and supplies over the pass.

A heavyset customs officer arrived in a pickup. He was Hawaiian and very friendly. He said he would drive us to Sandy Grunow's Sergeant Preston Lodge when we finished filling out the forms.

The main reason I came to Skagway was to see my Yukon friend, Tall Sandy. Sandy used to live at Watson Lake and I flew her and her boyfriend, Bob, out to Stewart Lake in the Yukon on several occasions. Sandy loved to camp in the bush. She sends me a Christmas card every year and keeps in touch from time to time with letters.

"Sandy's doing a great job and has been doing a lot of remodeling at her Sergeant Preston Lodge," the customs officer said.

The airport is on the west side of Skagway, and beautiful glacier-covered mountains can be seen as you look south down the runway. These mountains rise sharply out of Taiya Inlet, southwest of town.

After filling out forms and purchasing a $25 decal that the customs officer insisted I buy for the plane, we climbed into his pickup and he drove us to Sandy's Sergeant Preston Lodge in Skagway.

We walked into the lobby of the cozy Sergeant Preston Lodge and there was "Tall Sandy."

"Hi Sandy, how are you doing?"

"Just fine, Larry. I didn't think I would ever see you here. After you called me a while back and said you planned on flying up soon, then didn't come, I didn't think I would see you."

"Well, it took longer than I thought to get here. Let's get some pictures, Sandy."

"Oh, I don't want my picture taken."

"Ah, come on."

"Well, okay."

Janey took a picture of Sandy and me outside of the Hotel in front of a sign that read "Sergeant Preston Lodge."

As usual, Sandy looked very striking in her long dress, similar to the style they wore here in town during the Gold Rush era of 1898. We walked to a nearby restaurant and had lunch as we caught up on news of the north. Sandy has been in Skagway for two years and she told me a bit about the town, which she thoroughly enjoys.

"Do you like it better than Watson Lake?"

"Yes, I do. It was time for a change."

I told Sandy about the time I spent at Watson Lake a few days before and about the people I saw: Jim and Stan, Lynn, and others we both knew. We had a good lunch and a nice visit, but it was too short.

Janey and I walked through town and she took some videos and pictures of several cruise ships that were tied up at Skagway's piers. The crowds off the ships were walking down the street and busily buying souvenirs.

In about 1983 I drove to Prince Rupert, British Columbia with my son. We caught the ferry and departed for Juneau, Alaska. Scott spent that college summer vacation working as a builder in southeast Alaska. I caught a small plane and flew to Skagway and overnighted there. I took pictures of the town and of the graveyard where the infamous con artist, Soapy Smith, was laid to rest after being shot by one of Skagway's leading citizens, Frank Reid.

Soapy also shot Frank Reid, who died later from his wounds. Soapy's grave had flowers on it during my stop, as I recall, but Frank Reid's grave seemed forgotten.

This picture was taken from downtown Skagway, where the cruise ships tied up (photo by Janey Youngblood).

Janey had visited Skagway several years ago on a cruise ship. We walked to a building that serves as an office for a flying service at the Skagway Airport. They have many Piper Cherokee airplanes which are used for flying tourists over nearby glaciers. It's unbelievable. A rush of tourists fill up the airplanes and they take off and land like a swarm of bumblebees, a continuous blur of airplanes, and then all is quiet until another group of tourists arrives from another ship.

CHAPTER 15

Return to Atlin

Icalled the Juneau Flight Service Station and filed a flight plan to Atlin, British Columbia. I taxied to the end of the runway and when it looked clear, I got out of there in a hurry! There were too many airplanes buzzing around without a control tower to suit me.

After lifting off, we flew over the ocean that begins at the south end of the runway. We made a climbing left turn over the water and headed north, following the Skagway River. Atlin is only fifty-seven air miles east of Skagway, but because of glacier-covered mountains the route I flew was farther.

Turquoise lakes and beautiful glacier-covered mountains surrounded us as we flew to Atlin Lake. We flew back over Tagish Lake and turned south as we reached Atlin Lake.

We then flew around the west side of Teresa Island on Atlin Lake, four miles southwest of the town of Atlin. Birch Mountain on Teresa Island is the highest mountain on any fresh water island in the world. The top of the mountain is covered with ice and snow and is 6,758 feet above sea level.

The late afternoon sun glistened on the water as we approached Atlin. We flew over the town of Atlin and circled over part of the airport, then landed into the wind on runway 18.

After tying up the plane I called Lyman Sands who, along with his many other hats, is also the customs officer. I was a bit concerned because the number that the Flight Service Station in Juneau gave me for the Atlin Customs was actually the wrong number. I called that number and it was a recording at a Customs Office that said to leave a message. Thinking it Atlin, I left a message and gave my ETA. You're required to contact Customs before you land; usually it's part of your flight plan, but not in Atlin--you have to call there by phone.

When Lyman arrived, I told him about the number and he said it was Prince Rupert. There wasn't a problem and Lyman gave us a ride to the Fireweed Inn.

Am sitting on the dock and the splash of the water is quieting. Birch Island rises majestically across the lake.

2020: *I met Herman Peterson by his Luscomb float plane that sits over at his dock. He couldn't quite remember who I was, until I told him I flew his Luscomb at Watson Lake in 1971. We talked about flying and the difficult areas we had flown. Herman is almost 80 years old but looks 60-65, has thick hair, and is in good shape. Nice man. Will take his picture tomorrow. I'm tired and want to get home tomorrow.*

After walking back to the Fireweed Inn, I read for a while before sleep.

August 3, 1993

0813: *In Lorrie's Bed and Breakfast kitchen enjoying the aroma of good coffee. The pot's percolating. Sun's shining through the window and there are bright colored flowers outside the alcove window.*

Looking west from Lorrie's place, you can see Atlin Mountain rising above the Lake on the western shore. Part of this mountain broke off and a huge gravel slide can be seen on the east side of the mountain.

This quaint town has some old historic buildings from the early days. There is an old jail which is all boarded up. An impressive old church that's been renovated and is in use sits two blocks from Lorrie's. The peaceful quiet and beauty of this place slowly entered my bones. I forgot about the crazy modern world and didn't care if I ever went back. One's system slows down and begins to adapt to a different pace of life. I remember when I lived in the Yukon, we referred to a trip out of the territory as going to the outside.

The town of Atlin was born during the Gold Rush fever of 1898 when two prospectors, Fritz Miller and Kenny McLaren, discovered gold on Pine Creek. Within a year, over 10,000 rushed into the area looking for gold. Atlin became the center of commerce, providing the hardy pioneers with the service they required.

The early gold seekers called Atlin paradise and the tourists of the 1920s and 1930s called it the Switzerland of North America.

The movie "Never Cry Wolf" was filmed in the town of Atlin. The scene with the Beaver ski plane landing on a frozen wilderness lake is actually Atlin Lake and it was taken in front of the town.

The large boat MV Tarahne was built in 1916 for freight and to haul visitors across the lake. For twenty years, this vessel plied the waters of Atlin Lake, giving all those on board wonderful views of glacier-covered mountains and cascading streams.

We walked up beside the Tarahne, which was pulled on shore, and looked at this once stately boat. It must have some interesting stories and experiences to tell, if only it could speak, and I could feel the presence of the past.

Atlin can be reached from the Alaska Highway at Whitehorse, which is 110 miles away. The locals said it's a four-hour drive. Watson Lake is 285 miles away. Skagway by road is 160 miles, but it's only 57 air miles. Vancouver, B.C. is a 1,770-mile drive.

We did some sightseeing and then walked over to Herman Peterson's home by the shores of Atlin Lake. Janey and I decided it was time to get some videos of Herman and his airplanes and take him up on the invitation to see his biplane.

It was about 0930 when we walked over to the Peterson's home. I introduced Janey to Herman and we both met his wife, Dorris, who goes by the nickname of Suzy. Herman and I walked out on his dock to look at his Luscomb float plane. Janey and Suzy went into the house.

Well, as all pilots do, we began talking about some of our flying adventures when we flew in the bush for a living. Herman is a walking history of an earlier era and he told me the following:

He came to Carcross, Yukon Territory, February 11, 1942. Carcross is thirty-nine miles southeast of Whitehorse. Herman flew a Fairchild 71 eight years for George Simmons' Northern Airways, Ltd., at Carcross. He flew for the Canol Pipeline Project in the early forties during World War II. It was a pipeline built from the Norman Wells Oil Refinery, located on the Mackenzie

Susie Peterson, 82, and Herman Peterson, 79, are standing by Herman's Luscomb, which has a 150-horsepower engine. This picture was taken in Atlin, B.C., in 1993.

River in the Northwest Territories, to the new Alaska Highway and on to Whitehorse, I believe. I flew over the old Canol Pipeline for many miles, and used it as a landmark when I was a bush pilot.

He flew an Aeronca Sedan, a four-place airplane, for a time. Herman also had his own flying service at Atlin for many years, including a helicopter and helicopter base. Herman began his own flying company called Coast Range Airways, Ltd., in 1950 and operated it until 1967, some seventeen years. He purchased a new Bell G-U helicopter RQM. I believe Al Pelshay flew this helicopter for Herman.

In 1956, he purchased a brand-new Beaver CF-ITU and in 1957 bought another new Beaver, CF-JPM. In 1964, Herman purchased a used Otter CF-SUB from the Air Force. It was #8 off the assembly line and had low hours on it.

In 1967, Trans Turbo Air purchased Herman's fixed wing operation as well as his helicopter base.

Herman Peterson and Larry Whitesitt are standing beneath the wing of Herman's Luscomb seaplane. In the background is Birch Mountain on Teresa Island, which is the highest island mountain on a freshwater lake in the world, and to the right are the coastal mountains.

In 1918, Herman saw his first airplane, a Curtis Jenny, and his first ride was in a Gypsy Moth. He bought a Simon Sparton for $250 in 1934. It had a 115-horsepower engine and a wooden prop. Herman said he used the Otter for water-bombing fires. They installed a center water tank. I told him about my water-bombing experience with a Beaver on floats in 1970.

In 1943, Herman Peterson obtained his engineer's license (airplane mechanic) after a three-year apprenticeship. One of his hobbies is making violins.

"He's a mechanical genius and inventor," Lyman Sands at Atlin told me. "Some big company should have put Herman on their payroll and just let him use his creative talents as an inventor."

Besides the fact that Herman is an interesting bush pilot and had a lot of interesting stories to share, the thing that I liked most about him was his kind heart and gentle ways.

We went looking for Janey and Suzy and found them in Suzy's greenhouse looking at her tomatoes. Because of early frosts, tomatoes and other vegetables have to be grown in greenhouses at Atlin.

We all walked out on the dock and Janey began taking videos of Herman, Suzy and me next to the Luscomb. I patted Herman's head and said to Suzy, "Look, he's got a full head of hair."

She said, rather seriously, "When he loses his hair, I'm going to leave him."

I laughed at her wry humor. Petite Suzy is 82, but looks much younger. They are both in tiptop condition and do a lot of walking. Herman patted his flat stomach and said, "I'm in good shape."

After the filming, Herman said he would drive us to the airport and show us his pride and joy, a Smith biwing home-built that he constructed himself, and named Suzy. Suzy, his wife, said, "I'm not sure which Suzy he loves the most!"

We said our goodbyes to our host, Lorrie O'Neill, and put our baggage in the back of Herman's pickup. Lassie, Herman's beloved dog, sat on my lap in the front seat because I was sitting in her seat and she needed to put her nose out the window. Janey sat in the back jump seat.

We spent an hour at the airport looking at the well-constructed Smith biplane and then walked to the terminal building to file a flight plan by phone. After we said our goodbyes to Herman Peterson, I called the Whitehorse Flight Service Station and filed a flight plan to Smithers, B.C., with a stop at Dease Lake for fuel. After doing a good preflight check, we climbed in our faithful ship and started the engine. We taxied to a concrete pad by the runway and did the run-up, then taxied onto runway 18. We lifted off runway 18 at 1405 and left Atlin, Gem of the North, behind.

CHAPTER 16

Wilderness Flight Home

After lifting off runway 18 and flying south for a few minutes to gain a safe altitude, we banked left to the new heading of 90° that would take us across a friendly wilderness to our next fuel stop, Dease Lake, 152 miles away. Surprise Lake was north off the port wing as I began writing in my journal:

> 1427: *By Llangorse Lake, about 28 miles from Atlin. Bell Lake is off the starboard wing. Beautiful day wilderness below, a pleasant wilderness.*

> 1451: *By Prairie Lake a northern wilderness.*

> 1500: *By Granite and Tachilta Lakes.*

We flew over the north end of Dease Lake and around a mountain to line up with runway 20 at the Dease Lake Airport, where we landed for fuel. After topping the tanks and drinking a cup of coffee, we departed for Smithers, British Columbia, where we planned to overnight. Our new heading was 109°, which would take us to Kitchener and Tatlatui lakes where I wanted to get some pictures. Kitchener Lake was 137 miles and Smithers another 170 miles. We crossed the Stikine River after flying some fifty miles and flew east of Coldfish Lake, but couldn't see it because of mountains. We were flying over the east side of the Spatsizi wilderness area.

This is a picture of Kitchener Lake in B.C., where Larry flew his mother and father, Kathy and Scott on a fishing trip in the late 1960s.

I used to fly into Coldfish Lake for the outfitter Tommy Walker in 1967. After he retired from outfitting in 1968, he spent a lot of time persuading the British Columbia government to make the area around Coldfish Lake and the Northern Spatsizi Country a protected wilderness area. I remember his white hair and Tommy standing at the dock at his Coldfish Camp to help with the plane.

1717: *8,350 feet over the Stikine River, with wilderness as far as I can see. Back where I flew for Omineca Air Service in the late 1960s.*

1728: *7,850 feet over the Spatsizi Wilderness Area.*

1741: *Over Laslui Lake in the Spatsizi Wilderness Park.*

Fifteen miles northeast of Laslui Lake is Metsantan Lake and an abandoned Indian village site on the shores of that lake. I once flew in there with the Cessna 185 float plane CF-OXE to take pictures. In each log cabin we saw a gold pan hanging on the wall. A larger log building had old school primers, a place where the Indian children discovered other worlds outside their village. There were no roads, only wilderness in every direction.

This is a vast wilderness and I feel quite alone in this uninhabited land. We flew on and on and on. It didn't seem as if Kitchener Lake was

Larry's father, mother, wife and son fishing for rainbow trout on Kitchener Lake in B.C. They caught numerous rainbow trout from 2 to 4 pounds.

going to appear, but I continued to fly the heading.

Finally, I saw one end of a lake far off and it was Kitchener Lake, which is about ten miles long. The day was sunny and bright and the lake a beautiful blue with glassy calm surface. Fair-weather puffy cumulus clouds reflected in the transparent water. It was 1810 as I flew over the lake.

We circled over a sandy shore where Stalk Creek, which runs out of nearby Stalk Lake, enters Kitchener Lake on the north side. Tears came to my eyes and I choked up as I looked at the place where my father, mother, Kathy, six-year-old Scott and I had fished. We flew the Cessna 185 CF-OXE to Kitchener and heeled the floats up on the sandy beach. We all had fun that day as we caught a lot of trout.

My parents talked about that flight many times and they said the highlight of their year was the summer vacations they spent with us in Canada. Dad and Mom would take Scott fishing. He was their first grandson. Now my parents are gone and Scott is thirty-three years old. My, how fast time goes. Fond memories of this flight with my parents, Kathy and Scott are mine to hold.

After circling and taking pictures of Kitchener Lake, we flew a few miles south over Tatlatui Lake, from the northeast end to the south of the lake. This lake is twelve miles long and on the southeast side was some swamp land. Two moose were wading in the water. I descended low and circled so Janey could get pictures.

We circled several times, went over a high ridge, and into the next valley south over Thutade Creek. Thutade Lake, the headwaters of the mighty Mackenzie River, was two miles east. This is quite a large lake, some twenty-eight miles long, and is shaped like a bow. The last time I flew over this wilderness area was in 1969, when I flew out of McClure Lake as a bush pilot.

We flew south by the north end of Bear Lake and then headed for Fort Babine, at the north end of Babine Lake. Babine Lake is forty-three miles long. Takla Landing on Takla Lake is 14 miles northeast of Fort Babine. I flew the mail to both Fort Babine and Takla Landing in 1967, 1968, and 1969. At that time there were no roads to either place and the mail run was an enjoyable flight because of the scenery and also the interaction with the Indians of both villages. I learned much from these people and their unique, simple way of life.

1907: Can see Babine Lake ahead. Mt. Horetzky, an old flying landmark, is just ahead. This mountain stands alone above the valley floor. Fort Babine is ahead.

Nilkitkwa Lake is just north of Babine Lake, and the Babine River joins both lakes. Salmon swim up the river to Babine Lake. I remember that when I flew the mail into Fort Babine, the Indians could be seen drying salmon in large numbers.

We flew over the Babine River and circled Fort Babine several times so Janey could take photos. The old Hudson Bay Store with the red roof could be seen, as well as the store manager's old home. I believe all the bush stores are closed now and that Hudson's Bay only has large department stores in major cities. There is a bridge that crosses the Babine River just north of the fort so cars can drive to the village.

We flew down the lake a few miles south and then made a climbing right turn west, to Smithers. I remember one winter day as I was flying the Super Cub JUE on skis and had just started to fly over the east shore of the frozen lake near here, when seven wolves ran out from shore heading west across the lake. I flew toward a magnificent silver-colored wolf about twenty feet above the ice and as I got close I could tell the wolf was trying to figure

Larry's uncle (Jess McDaniel), father, Larry, Kathy, Scott and Gretchen (the dog) stand in front of Larry's log home in the Driftwood Valley. Larry helped build the home shortly after he began flying for Omineca Air Service in 1967.

out which direction to turn. When I was about thirty feet away, this magnificent creature turned left as I flew by.

I can still see in the mist of memories this wolf running full out, with a magnificent stride, a beautiful body, and a thick silver coat. Wolves are my favorite wild animal. Often in the winter while flying across the wilderness with a ski plane, I would see large packs of wolves sometimes twenty or more. Some were black, a few white, but mostly they were silver.

We fly between some mountains and over a pass, and majestic Hudson Bay Glacier slides into view. The Bulkley River winds lazily through a fertile green valley lined with many farms. The air is smooth as silk. As we descend toward the Smithers Airport, the town comes into view just east of Hudson Bay Glacier.

The peace and serenity I discovered in 1964, over twenty-nine years ago when I drove through this valley with my family for the first time as landed immigrants, fills my being once again and it feels good to be coming back.

This dream to go north, build a log cabin in the wilderness, and live off the land began in high school and was completed in this area with my family and high school buddy Jim Goerz, who built a log cabin near Smithers. Sometimes Jim would go along on flights with me.

Larry is standing next to the Cessna 185 CF-OXE on Takla Lake shortly after
the plane crashed on April 8, 1969. Later inspection found that a supporting
component to the landing gear had a hairline crack.

One flight that Jim and I shared into the wilderness stands out. On April
8, 1969, I prepared for a flight in the ski-equipped Cessna 185 CF-OXE to
Takla Post. Jack Newcomb wanted me to fly in some groceries and supplies
to his trading post store. This store was formerly a Hudson Bay trading post
and traded with the Takla Post Indians who had a village there. I invited Jim
to go along, as it was only a forty-minute flight, a quick turnaround, and then
the return flight   about two hours total. Jim mentioned he had to work that
afternoon, in about three hours.

"No problem, Jim," I told him, "We'll be back in plenty of time."

We lifted off the snow-packed strip at McClure Lake, flew through
Chapman Pass and over Babine Lake, then came in for a normal landing at
Takla Lake beside the Indian village of Takla Post. Touchdown was smooth
and all seemed normal.

After about a hundred feet, the plane started turning left on the ice. I
tried to correct the turn with the right rudder, but it had no effect and then the
right wing struck the ice as the right landing gear buckled under the plane.
Gas poured all over our clothes.

I yelled, "Let's get out of here, Jim!" The door was jammed from the
impact, gas from the wing tank was pouring on us and on the hot engine.
Panic set in as I thought of fire and getting burned alive; the thing pilots dread
the most. After several tries, I finally kicked the door open and we ran across
the ice, expecting an explosion.

All was quiet as we caught our breath. The right wing was bent up on the ice about eight feet from the wing tip. The prop was bent backwards toward the cockpit and the horizontal stabilizer on the right side was bent on the end. I had no idea what happened. A fine fix . . . we were about sixty miles from home and Jim had to get to work in a couple of hours.

Our two-hour trip took a couple of days. We were finally picked up by another ski plane and the Cessna 185 CF-OXE was flown out by helicopter. It was sold, rebuilt, and eventually ended up in the bottom of the ocean, I was told. Investigation revealed that a supporting component inside the fuselage had a hairline crack and it just let go at that particular time. The boss said it wasn't my fault and didn't hold it against me since I had no control over structural failure. I was somewhat shaken up, having never been involved in an accident before.

A few miles south of here is McClure Lake, where I had my first flying job as a bush pilot. On my first flight as a commercial pilot, I flew Carl Faye in the float-equipped Piper Super Cub JUE to Alice Arm, an inlet off the Pacific Ocean north of Prince Rupert. What a thrill and how excited I was to get paid for doing what I loved. My first love in life was airplanes and the wonder of flight is a love affair that began when I was a very small boy.

"Smithers Radio, this is Cessna November 62731."

"Cessna 62731, Smithers Radio, go ahead."

"Roger. I'm ten miles northeast inbound for the airport."

"731, Smithers Radio, the wind is calm, favoring runway 32."

"Okay, I'll make a right hand base for runway 32."

"731, Smithers Radio give me a call on final."

"Okay, 731."

Descending toward the airport, I had many feelings and good memories of other flights into this airport and on floats to nearby McClure Lake. At one time I flew my Aeronca Chief CF-UVX into this airport and kept it here until I sold it to some local pilots.

"Smithers Radio, 731 turning final for runway 32."

"731 Smithers Radio check you're turning final no reported traffic."

The air was smooth and the approach good. The tires made a slight "erk-erk" as they touched the runway.

"Smithers Radio, 731, please close my flight plan."

"731, Smithers Radio, your flight plan is now closed."

"Thank you, good day, sir."

Janey called the Hudson Bay Lodge and they said they would send someone to get us. Sitting on a patch of grass in front of the airport terminal building, many memories were reawakened at this place where I once made my home. The country looks much the same with the peaceful Bulkley Valley, the magnificent Hudson Bay Glacier towering over the town and the rugged glacier-covered mountains in most directions.

A van drove up and a friendly woman took us to the Hudson Bay Lodge.

We walked the streets of Smithers at about 2200 and rented a VCR player to attach to the TV so we could watch footage that Janey had taken of our trip. At the Lodge, we watched videos of our flight until we could no longer stay awake.

August 4, 1993-0837: *Outside, the sky is blue and the sun bright as I contemplate the flight to Williams Lake and Felts Field in Spokane. Should take about six hours, including the fuel stop at Williams Lake.*

After arising, we ate breakfast at the restaurant in the lodge. A man drove us in the lodge van to the Smithers Airport. After fueling, I walked to the Flight Service Station and filed a flight plan to Felts Field, Spokane, Washington, with a fuel stop at Williams Lake.

Smithers Airport doesn't have a control tower. The altitude is 1,712 feet ASL and the runway is 5,000 feet long.

We climbed aboard our plane and taxied toward the runway. After the run-up and check for traffic, we rolled out on runway 14 and departed for Williams Lake, lifting off at 1115 into a hazy sky on a heading of 102°. Williams Lake is 276 air miles from Smithers. Smithers passed beneath our wings and next we flew over my old base at Tyee Lake, also known as McClure Lake, and noticed a few float planes. We flew by Tchesinkut Lake, where Omineca Air Service had their other seaplane base. The company was sold to Trans-Provincial Air Service, in the 1970s.

The steady drone of the engine, and the country below slowly sliding by, bring back memories of the days I flew over this country as a bush pilot in the 1960s. Many changes have taken place since then. Kathryn and I were divorced in 1971.

Scott was a young boy then and now he has a son of his own. Life seems complete with the birth of my grandson Daniel. I recall a recent hike with Daniel on my back when he let out a loud "WHEEEE" as we hit the trail by

This is the Omineca Air Service seaplane base at Tyee Lake (also known as McClure Lake), where Larry landed his first job as a commercial pilot. In the foreground is a Piper Super Cub CF-JUE in which he made his first flight to Alice Arm. Behind the Piper is a Beaver and two Otters.

their new country home near Twin Lakes, Idaho. Scott lives about twenty-five miles from Spokane, where he works for a large architectural firm.

A few miles south of Tchesinkut Lake, we cross over Francois Lake at 1204. This lake is sixty-two air miles long but with the many bends, it is longer. About fifty miles south of Francois Lake, we passed by Kenney Dam at 1224. This dam backs up a huge waterway, consisting of Ootsa, Eutsuk, and smaller lakes that are all connected, making a circle some 250 miles long. Kenney Dam was created to provide electricity for an aluminum company at Kitimat, which is located at the head of an inlet off the Pacific Ocean.

We crossed the Fraser River near a bend in the river that was in line with the Williams Lake Airport, according to my reading of the sectional chart. I called the Williams Lake Radio on 126.7 and told them I was estimating the airport in five minutes and that my position was northwest of the airport. What I thought was the airport turned out to be farm buildings and a large field. After five minutes, a voice came over the earphones.

"Cessna 62731, what's your position now?"

"Williams Lake Radio, Cessna 62731. I'm looking for the airport. Haven't spotted it yet."

How embarrassing, I thought, as I scanned the countryside looking for the elusive airport. Finally, the Williams Lake Radio operator told me to press and hold my mike button down so he could get a fix on the airplane, and I quickly complied.

"Cessna 62731, fly a heading of 251° and you should see the airport shortly, you're only a short distance away."

"Okay, thanks, 731." Sure enough, this red-faced pilot spotted the airport about four miles northwest.

"Williams Lake Radio 731 I now have the airport in sight. I'm really embarrassed, I've flown all over the Yukon and I can't find the Williams Lake Airport."

"Oh, don't feel bad it happens a lot we're hard to see," came the friendly reply.

I've been to this airport several times before and never had a problem spotting the field. It was a good lesson to stay alert even when you think you know your exact position. Fatigue and not paying close attention the last few minutes before arriving in the vicinity of the airport help contribute to flying just a bit north of the field and missing it completely.

But it was a good lesson and a good ego deflator. A pilot can't be too careful. This time I had plenty of fuel and could have flown back to the Fraser River, followed it down river to the town of Williams Lake and followed the road to the airport, but another time it could be a serious problem.

After landing, I topped the fuel tanks, then visited a few minutes with the radio operator at the Flight Service Station and thanked him for his help in finding the elusive airport. He was a friendly and talkative chap. Williams Lake airport has an elevation of 3,085 feet and the paved runway is 7,000 feet long. The airport frequency is 122.3 and of course it has the standard 126.7, which all Canadian Flight Service Stations monitor.

We lifted off runway 11 on course to Felts Field, which is 374 air miles southeast. Sixty-one miles out of Williams Lake, about halfway to Kamloops, we passed over the green waters of Green Lake, a good landmark. At 1529, we were over the city of Kamloops, British Columbia, and thirty-five miles farther, Douglas Lake was below us.

At 1604, we passed Kelowna at an altitude of 8,750 feet. Southeast of this rapidly growing city, which straddles beautiful Lake Okanogan, a voice in my earphones brought me to attention.

"Cessna November 62731 Penticton Radio."

"Penticton Radio Cessna 62731, go ahead."

"731, Penticton Radio, you're to fly direct to Spokane International

Airport to clear customs."

"Okay, fly direct to Spokane International Airport to clear Customs, 731."

Boy, that was one message I didn't want to receive. I was looking forward to flying direct to Felts Field, landing, tying down my ship and heading home for a hot shower and a good night's sleep in my own bed.

We crossed the border into Washington state near Grand Forks, British Columbia, and soon flew over the large body of water called Roosevelt Lake, near the town of Kettle Falls. About 20 miles out, I called Spokane Approach Control, after listening to a lot of traffic on the radio coming and going to Spokane International Airport. Spokane Approach Control had difficulty hearing me on the radio, so I told them I didn't wish to land there.

"Which airport do you prefer?"

"Felts Field," I quickly replied.

"Okay, you're cleared, fly direct to Felts Field."

I was relieved, having never flown a plane into Spokane International Airport, which is quite busy at times. I didn't want to make a stupid mistake, which would have been easy to do as I was quite tired. I called the Flight Service Station at Felts Field, explained the problem with the radio and asked if they would contact Customs and ask them to meet me at Felts.

A few minutes later, they came back on the radio and said Customs would meet me at Felts, but that I would have to wait a short while after I landed until Customs arrived at the field. I contacted Felts Tower about ten miles north of the airport, reported my position and was instructed to report downwind for runway 3 left. We entered the downwind leg over a ridge about one mile east of Beacon Hill.

Another pilot was talking to the tower and I waited about one minute until the frequency was clear, then pressed the black mike button on the control column and spoke into the mike, which is part of the headphone set.

"Felts Tower, Cessna 731 is downwind for runway 3 left."

"731, Felts Tower, you are No. 2 to land, after the Red Baron. Report when turning final."

"Okay, I'm No. 2, I have the other airplane in sight, report on final, 731."

The Red Baron is a bi-wing stunt plane and the pilot has been practicing for an upcoming air show. I watch as the Red Baron touches down and taxies off the runway. The air is smooth as I turn final.

"Felts Tower, 731 is turning final for runway 3 left."

"731, you're cleared to land."

"Okay, 731 cleared to land, thank you, sir!"

"Cleared to land" was music to my ears.

With full flaps and approach speed of sixty knots, a familiar scene unfolds at this special place where my first flying lesson began in the late 1950s, some thirty-four years ago. On that memorable day, Russ Swanson, who owned Mamer and Schreck Flying Service gave me my first hour of dual in his Aeronca Champ. We flew off a grass strip just south of the paved runway and Russ introduced me to the "mystery and marvel of flight," which in time became a way of life.

A deep and wondrous feeling of completeness and awe fills my cockpit world as the runway approaches. When I think of all the places I've been and the adventures I've experienced across the vast north in the past seven days, it's as though I've been in a wonderful dream and that it really didn't happen.

My mind returns again and again to that incredible northern beauty called Atlin Lake. Plans are beginning to form as I dream of returning to the peaceful waters of that great lake and the surrounding wilderness where I can concentrate on the important issues of life: watching loons and listening to their lonely haunting cry, writing, and fishing for huge trout in those sparkling clear waters.

Rounding out above the runway numbers, we float a short distance and complete this northern flight of dreams with a smooth, happy landing.

Epilogue

The familiar, reassuring roar of the nine-cylinder, 450-horsepower Pratt and Whitney radial engine filled the cockpit. The blue and white de Havilland Beaver float plane raced across Lake Coeur d'Alene, then gracefully lifted into the bright summer skies on Thursday, July 11, 1996.

Daniel, my three and one-half-year-old grandson, sat on his father Scott's lap in the right-hand copilot's seat as he experienced his first airplane ride. A wide grin and look of awe spread across his happy face. Kaitlyn, my two and one-half-year-old granddaughter, sat between her mother Stacy (who was pregnant with Gavin) and me in the middle bench seat behind the pilot, Grant Brooks. A tear ran down her cheek but she kept her thoughts quietly to herself. Janey Youngblood filmed the flight from the backseat.

We circled over the lake cabin of my late grandfather, William Charles Rydblom, located near the southern end of Lake Coeur d'Alene across from Harrison, Idaho. Daniel caught two perch with me not far from the cabin, where we tied up a boat to a log piling near the mouth of the Coeur d'Alene River after visiting the cabin during that special summer of 1996. Earlier in the year I took him fishing and watched the delight on his face as he caught his first fish, the colorful rainbow trout.

We were capturing this first airplane ride on video. After a smooth landing on the lake by the seaplane base I walked along the beach with Daniel. He noticed the Beaver circling overhead on another flight.

"Grandpa, were we that high?" he asked.

"We were higher than that," I replied, and a warm smile spread across his face.

During that special summer of 1996, Kaitlyn, Daniel and I hiked up

Pilot Grant Brooks, Scott (holding Daniel), Stacy (at left), Kaitlyn and Larry are inside Bill Brooks Beaver float plane, flying over Lake Coeur d'Alene.

Liberty Creek Trail to Split Island Crossing. We experienced our first campfire together, as we roasted wieners and marshmallows. After eating a delicious meal of hot dogs, I said, "We'd better head back down the trail to the car. It's almost dark."

"Grandpa, you promised to tell a story," Daniel said. And so began our ritual of telling grizzly bear stories of the far north around the campfire. After many stories we headed down the trail. Kaitlyn rode on my shoulders and Daniel held my hand tightly as he walked close behind me.

"What's that, grandpa?" he asked as he heard a sound in the dark woods. No doubt he was thinking about a grizzly bear.

"Oh, probably a deer, Daniel," I replied, trying to calm his fears.

Kaitlyn, Daniel and I have forced a special bond as we hike trails in eastern Washington and northern Idaho and tell tales of the north around a campfire. Kaitlyn is a kind, loving child with a motherly manner, always looking out for other people, dogs, cats and goldfish. Her great love is horses, and she is saving money to buy a horse of her own. I watched her the first time she got on a horse and it was the most natural event, as though she were born on a horse.

My youngest grandson Gavin picked out a huge douglas fir on the east side of Liberty Creek trail as his special hugging tree. It is just a short

Daniel Whitesitt and Joshua and Jeremiah Schreindl are walking under the wing of the blue and white Beaver. Jeremiah read Larry's book and wrote him a letter and asked about the Red Beaver. Larry and Jeremiah became friends and Larry invited him to fly in this Beaver on August 30, 2000, to celebrate his 13th birthday.

distance up the trail from the rest of our own hugging trees. Gavin has a great sense of humor and around the dinner table he usually gets everyone laughing.

Scott is one of the principals of ALSC Architectural Firm in Spokane, Washington, and has been busy the past few years doing architectural work for the Air Force. He was the design architect for the new home and garden center, part of the Base Exchange at Hickam Air Force Base in Hawaii and received a National Honor Award from the Air Force for this project, presented by General Lupe. They put a picture of the Hickam project on the front of the Air Force Architect Magazine. Later, he was the design architect for the newly constructed Home & Garden Center at McChord Air Force Base, Tacoma, Washington, and was the design architect on the new mini-mall and Base Exchange recently completed at Tinker Air Force Base in Oklahoma. Scott designed and helped build a Habitat for Humanity home on the north side of Spokane. Scott's beautiful wife, Stacy, is a super, full-time mother and homemaker. Her children adore her.

Scott designed and built with his own hands a unique two-story home on about 12 acres. Their home sits on a knoll in Northern Idaho. Large cedar, fir, and pine line the creek and surround the home.

Larry, Stacy, Daniel, Kaitlyn and Gavin Whitesitt pose for a picture after the August 30, 2000, flight in the blue and white Beaver.

In late September, 1996, there was a message on my answering service. Bob Close of Watson Lake Flying Service wanted me to call. When I returned his call, he told me a story. "A pilot they hired from England was flying the Red Beaver CF-IBP float plane and crashed into a mountain. The pilot was killed and the Red Beaver exploded." I told Bob how sorry I was to hear about this tragic accident.

Sometime after hearing about the Red Beaver's final flight, I talked to Darell Nelson, a northern pilot who flies his own Maul float plane and owned Northwest Territory Outfitters. He said the Red Beaver pilot was very cautious and would circle before landing at his camp. He related a story told to him by one of the owners of Watson Lake Flying service. Darell said the pilot was flying for an outfitter in Frank Stewart's old hunting area. Some local hunters asked if he would move their gear to another lake and the pilot agreed. Flying alone, he got into a snowstorm and flew up the wrong canyon. It was too steep for the Beaver to climb out and they crashed into the mountainside.

The saga of the Red Beaver CF-IBP has come to an end. The remarkable airplane, my favorite ship of all time, lies on a wilderness mountain in Northwestern British Columbia, by a place called Oblique Lake. So long, my faithful friend.

Daniel Whitesitt is paddling his kayak in the channel between Priest Lake and Upper Priest Lake. Daniel and Larry paddled their new Old Town Loon Kayaks to Upper Priest Lake for a two-day camping trip, where they swam and, of course, went fishing.

At 0500, Wednesday, August 25, 1999, the week before my grandson Daniel began the first grade in Rathdrum, Idaho, we began a new adventure. After a hearty breakfast of hot oatmeal cereal topped with honey, bananas and milk, we climbed into my van and left my apartment in the Spokane Valley. We drove north about 70 miles to the Beaver Creek Portage, which is located about a quarter of a mile north of Priest Lake.

After loading the gear in the bow and stem, we slid into the compact, but comfortable kayak. I thought we might sink to the bottom but we had several inches of freeboard. We pushed off from shore, Daniel, who was sitting in front, began paddling and I paddled in sync with him. The kayak paddles have blades at both ends and the rolling motion as you dip one paddle and then the other is very natural and comfortable. It's much easier to paddle than a canoe, especially for one person, and it tracks in a fairly straight line. The lower half of your body is below the water line, as you sit in a seat on the bottom of the craft, and the stability is excellent. Our necessities of life — food, clothing, shelter, and transportation — were in a compact, efficient craft and the freedom was exhilarating. It was kind of like slipping into my first airplane, a Piper J-3 Cub, a snug cockpit world, but very comfortable.

The water was very clear and we could see the bottom. Fish jumped, and the thick forest lined the shore as we quietly slipped through the water and deeper into a pristine wilderness area. Daniel was a strong paddler and as always a cheerful, warm-hearted companion. He reminds me so much of his father, Scott, who as a boy was my cheerful companion on northern trails

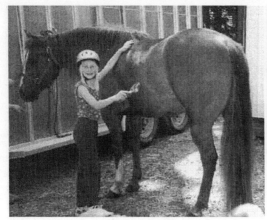

Kaitlyn loves horses and is saving her money to buy one. Gavin's pal is Hunter Whitesitt, a yellow lab.

and co-pilot as we flew float planes across the northern Canadian wilderness.

After about two miles, we merged with Upper Priest Lake and pulled up to a sandy beach and ate peanut butter and honey on honey-wheat bread, washed down with water. After a short lunch, we were ready to continue this adventure. We pushed off from shore and began paddling toward the far northwest end of Upper Priest Lake, about four miles away. A tail wind helped push us along. The scenery was spectacular as the forested shores rose upward and merged with towering mountains, which surrounded the lake. We found a sandy beach where we decided to set up camp. After unloading the kayak, we carried it up the beach and turned it over by some trees where the forest began.

"Daniel, there are grizzly bears and mountain caribou in this wilderness area," I said.

Daniel looked up at me and said, "Are there really grizzly bears here?"

"Yes," I replied.

We found a trail about 100 feet from shore and Daniel said, "Grandpa, let's hike on the trail!"

We followed the trail around the lake on an easterly heading and soon met a dog and a colorful man pushing a mountain bike. His name was Steven Marston and he said, "I came off Hugh's Mountain Lookout to check on a fire down the lake and am heading back to the lookout. A firefighting crew is on the fire. They have a pump running down by the lake and have a hose to the fire."

We noticed their boat pulled up to the shore as we paddled down the lake. Shortly after leaving Steven, we passed two dogs and two children and then we met a friendly woman named Jill Cobb. She said, "Have you seen two children with two dogs?"

"Yes," I replied. "We just passed them a little ways back."

"Oh good, now I know where my children are," she said. She said her husband David was back at their campsite along the lake and they were spending a week tent camping with their children, Paul and Robin, before school started. Jill is a hydrologist and her husband David is a forester. They both work for the Priest Lake Ranger District.

Daniel and I continued our hike and soon came to the Cobb family campsite. David, who was relaxed and reading a book, introduced himself He stands about 6-foot-5, on a lean frame, and looks like a man who has spent his life in the outdoors. He laughed when he pointed out his motor boat, a canoe and two kayaks, as he said, "I'm kind of big to get into the kayaks any more and use the motor boat."

After a short time, we left the Cobb family and walked back toward our campsite. After arriving back at our campsite, we tried to contact Daniel's mother Stacy on her cell phone, which I borrowed from her. We agreed to give her a call if we decided to stay overnight. However, we couldn't get through on the phone, probably because the surrounding mountains cut off the reception.

Daniel said, "Grandpa, I think mom will worry about us if we stay overnight and can't tell her."

We both worried about what to do. I really wanted to stay, but decided the right thing to do would be to go home that day.

After a bite to eat, we loaded our gear one more time in the kayak and pushed off into the lake. A brisk headwind fought us all the way down the lake.

"Grandpa, it's so far to the other end of the lake," Daniel said.

"Yes, but if we just keep paddling, we'll get there before too long," I said. At times, I told Daniel to rest and when he began paddling, I could notice a distinct increase in our forward speed. He is a strong paddler.

After a time, we came to the channel and then, still fighting a headwind, we arrived at the Beaver Creek portage. We ate some cheese and bread, before carrying the kayak and gear on the trail up the hill to the van. We were two, wet, tired boys, but we experienced a wonderful adventure that day.

We are thinking about purchasing a larger, two-place, Old Town kayak, called a Loon 160, next summer, so we can do some serious kayak camping.

A short time after our kayak trip, I received in the mail an envelope with a boy scout knife and a letter from Steven Marston. He said, "I found this knife on that trail where we met and I'm sure you will find the rightful owner. I drove to Priest Lake Ranger District Office with my sister Nancy and showed the knife to Jill Cobb.

"Oh, it's my son Paul's knife and he was so sad when he lost it," Jill said. "I know he'll be happy to get it back."

Later I received a nice thank you card from Jill Cobb which said, "I wish you could have seen Paul's face when he was reunited with his cherished pocketknife. I told Dave the whole story and he, too, found it remarkable."

Paul said in the card, "Dear Mr. Whitesitt, Thank you for finding my pocketknife. I missed it."

A couple of weeks or so after our wilderness adventure, Daniel said, "Grandpa, I dreamed we were in the kayak, flying through the air."

The following summer, Daniel and I paddled in our brand new Old Town Loon kayaks back up to Upper Priest Lake and spent two nights in a tent. We went swimming about a dozen times on a hot summer day, and of course we did some fishing.

Name Index

A

Adams, Tim, 36
Ahern, Shannon, 35
Angier, Vena and Bradford, 26

B

Ball, Dennis, 160
Barstow, Jill, 38
Bear, Fred, 44
Benedict, Frank, 113
Bissell, Angie, 87
Boone, Daniel, 44
Bowdey, Mr. and Mrs., 26, 49-51, 60
Bridcut, Stan, 127, 128, 131, 144
Brooks, Bill, 64, 206
Brooks, Grant, 65, 205, 206
Brown, Ray and Mel, 38
Burdatta, Tom, 38

C

Callison, Dempsey, 161
Casey, Tom, 58, 59
Close, Bob, 36, 127, 208
Close, Jim, 127, 128, 130
Cobb, Jill, 211, 212
Collison, Marv, 36
Cooke, Frank, 164-166, 170
Craford, Edmund Omar, 84
Crockett, Davy, 44

D

Dalziel, George, 16, 17, 169
Davidson, John Oglivie, 165
Day, Fletcher, 21
Douglas, Sr., John, 115
Drift, Johnny, 130

E

Ellis, Bill, 125
Ellis, Lynn, 125
Eisenhower, President Dwight D., 83

F

Faille, Albert, 158
Farber, Florence, 62
Furlott, Nancy, 102

G

Gentry, Jay, 38
Goerz, Jim, 26, 28, 42, 49, 53, 54, 197

H

Harrison, Ernie, 17
Heston, Charlton, 41
Hill, Samuel, 77-79

Hyland, Steel, 20

I

Ide, Colburn, 27

K

Keen, Val, 36
Kennedy, President John F., 83
Kinzer, Mary, 38

L

Liming, Dennis and Marcia, 61
London, Jack, 140, 183
Love, Bill, 44

M

Maccoll, Doug, 111
Malesko, Steve, 156, 159
McCaully, Peggy, 59
McCook, Emil, 119
McDaniel, Jess, 196
McDaniel, JoAnn, 39
McLaughlin, Lee, 26, 49, 54, 59
McLaughlin, Lucille, 38
McLeod, Charlie, 150
Miller, Dan, 64
Miller, Joe, 84
Mitchell, Ben, 26, 49
Mitchell, Benny, 54
Morris, Patty, 48

N

Nelson, Darell, 37, 163

O

O'Brien, Wilbur, 37
O'Conner, Jack, 170

O'Harra, Chris, 35
O'Neill, Lorrie, 174, 176, 192
Olney, Chris, 38

P

Parker, Fess, 43, 44
Peterson, Herman, 174, 188, 190-192
Peterson, Susie, 190
Pickett, Nancy, 38
Poizer, John, 127

R

Rae, Dennis, 112
Riggs, Everett, 59
Roosevelt, President Teddy, 85
Rydblom, Grandpa William Charles, 104, 205

S

Sands, Ann, 176
Sands, Lyman, 176, 187, 191
Schreindl, Joshua and Jeremiah, 206
Slippy, Sue, 38
Smith, Charley, 17, 21
Smith, Mike, 117
Sprank, Lisa, 39
Spurling, Linda, 62
Stahnke, Paul, 129, 143
Swan, Walter, 85, 86
Swanson, Russ, 203

T

Tait, Jamie, 174, 175
Taylor, Don, 143
Thiboudeau, Jim, 124, 125, 127, 142

W

Walker, Tommy, 39, 194
Waulkonan, Wally, 127
White, Ernie and Eunice, 84

Whitesitt, Daniel, 5, 44, 75, 200, 205, 206, 208-212
Whitesitt, Gavin, 5, 205-208
Whitesitt, Kaitlyn, 5, 205, 206, 208, 210
Whitesitt, Kathy, 17, 25, 26, 28, 42, 59, 101, 104, 120, 194-196
Whitesitt, Larry, 3, 4, 10, 15, 19, 21, 24, 35, 38, 41, 44, 47, 49, 54, 58, 75, 80, 87, 99, 102, 107, 113, 117, 124, 125, 127, 130, 136, 148-152, 161, 166, 169, 170, 176, 185, 191, 194, 196, 197, 206, 208, 209, 217
Whitesitt, Scott, 5, 10, 14, 17-19, 25-28, 31-35, 40-42, 48, 49, 53, 57, 58, 63, 64, 73, 88-90, 93-95, 98, 100, 103-106, 120, 121, 128, 134, 142, 143, 148, 149, 165, 185, 194-196, 200, 201, 206, 207, 209
Whitesitt, Stacy, 5, 34, 35, 53, 57, 88, 90, 93,

103, 106, 205-208, 211
Wien, Jr., Noel, 59
Wien, Noel Merrill, 59
Winoski, Gene, 117
Wood, Alex, 36
Woolliams, Nina G., 115

Y

Youngblood, Janey, 9, 107, 108, 111, 117, 119, 121, 125-127, 129, 130, 137, 140, 147, 149, 158, 159, 161, 166, 174-176, 182, 185, 186, 189, 191, 192, 196, 200, 205

Subject Index

A

A-26 bomber, 140
Aeronca Champ, 203
Aeronca Chief, 28, 112, 199
Alaska, 1-3, 13, 16, 24, 37, 45, 48, 59, 62, 67,
  98, 100, 104, 116, 119, 121, 123, 125, 140,
  155, 163, 173, 176, 177, 182, 184, 185,
  189, 190
Alaska Airlines, 59
Alaska Highway, 13, 16, 119, 121, 125, 155,
  163, 189, 190
Alberta, 43, 87, 113
ALSC Architectural Firm, 207
American Export Airline, 65
Anderson Lake, 62
Apache Junction, 81
Arctic, 9, 13-16, 29, 31, 94, 100, 101, 119, 120,
  123, 133, 136, 137, 140
Arctic Circle, 14, 136
Arctic Ocean, 14, 15, 29, 94, 100, 123
At Home in the Woods, 26
Atlin, 8, 20, 157, 170, 171, 173-176, 179, 181,
  187-193, 204
Atlin Trading post, 176
Audubon Society, 107
Auntie's Bookstore, 35
Aztec, 112, 113, 134, 142, 161

B

B-25 bomber, 114
B. Dalton, 48
B.C. Yukon Air Service, 16, 125, 145, 163
Baird Glaciers, 24

bald eagle, 13, 88, 119
Barnstormers Lounge, 59
Barstow, 38, 68, 213
Bayview, 104, 105
Beacon Hill, 94, 203
Beaufort Sea, 13, 15, 120
Beech 18, 128, 142, 175
Bellevue, 32, 33, 41
Bennett Lake, 177, 178
Big Kalzas Lake, 134
Bisbee, 7, 81, 83-87
Black Mike's Hotel, 134
Boeing Field, 57, 58, 112, 113
Boeing Museum of Flight, 42, 58
Book and Game Store, 35
Book Warehouse, 87, 88
Bowser Lake, 23, 24
British Columbia, 1-3, 8, 13, 14, 16, 23, 24, 27,
  28, 36, 42, 43, 49, 53, 64, 91, 93, 95, 97,
  100, 108, 111-113, 115-120, 123, 125, 129,
  130, 155, 157, 161, 165, 173-175, 185,
  187, 193, 194, 202, 208, 228
British Yukon Navigation Company, 139
Bulkley River, 28, 197
Burns Lake, 27

C

California, 35, 43, 66, 67, 70, 71, 85, 97
Canada, 9, 14, 24, 25, 27, 29, 38, 43, 48, 49, 64,
  75, 78, 91, 93, 96, 98, 99, 101, 102, 108,
  109, 121, 165, 170, 182, 195, 228
Canby, 73
Canyonville, 71
caribou, 13, 15, 101, 111, 119, 154, 166, 210
Cassiar Mountains, 13, 120, 169

Celilo Falls, 72, 78, 118
Cessna, 9, 14, 22, 32, 36, 57, 58, 64, 70, 93, 94,
    98, 100, 101, 103, 107, 112, 117, 123, 126,
    129, 131, 143, 175, 194, 195, 197-199,
    201-203
Cessna *172*, 14, 93, 94, 107, 112
Cessna *185*, 32, 36, 57, 58, 64, 100, 103, 126,
    129, 131, 143, 175, 194, 195, 197-199
Cessna *206*, 64
Cessna *734*, 9, 22, 98, 101
Chewelah, 62, 102
Chillawack, 53
Coldfish Lake, 24, 193, 194
Colt Lake, 165, 170
Columbia River, 71, 72, 76, 78, 80, 118
Colville, 26, 61, 62, 108
Colville Indian Reservation, 108
Colville Rendezvous, 61, 62
Crater Lake, 74-76
Crater Lake National Park, 74
Crescent Lake, 50

D

Dawson City, 7, 15, 20, 133-140, 173, 177,
    183, 184
Dawson City Bed and Breakfast Inn, 137, 140
Deadmen Valley, 8, 133, 140, 145, 146,
    149-151, 153, 157, 160
Dease Lake, 14, 16, 17, 157, 159, 161, 169,
    171, 192, 193
Dease Lake Airport, 14, 16, 193
Dease River, 16
deer, 13, 62, 73, 95, 101, 102, 107, 119, 154,
    206
Deer Park Airport, 95
Dene Indians, 148
Denmark, 34
Diamond J Ranch, 165
Divide Lake, 163
Douglas Lake Cattle Company 115
Driftwood Valley, 28, 130, 197

E

Eagle River, 13, 16
Earn Lake, 134, 141

Edizza Peak, 22, 23
Edmonton, 50, 87

F

FAA, 113
Faucett Lookout, 104, 105
Felts Field, 9, 14, 28, 36, 93, 95, 107, 111, 200,
    202, 203
Felts Field Aviation, 93, 95
Finlay River, 13, 116-120
Fireweed Book Store, 36
Flat Creek, 147
Flight of the Red Beaver, 2, 9, 32, 33, 35-37,
    39, 40, 44, 48, 53, 58, 72, 73, 80, 81, 88,
    90, 91, 107, 134, 228
Fort Babine, 196
Fort Good Hope, 14
Fort Liard, 8, 113, 133, 150, 153, 155, 157,
    159, 161
Fort of the Forks, 14
Fort Simpson, 14, 150, 155, 161
Fort St. John, 14
Fort Ware, 117-119
Frances Lake, 141-143
Ft. Meyers, 31

G

Glacier National Park, 70, 88, 120
glaciers, 24, 51, 100, 175, 186
Gold Rush, 15, 134, 136, 140, 184, 185, 188
Goldendale, 67, 72, 76, 77, 79, 80
Grand Canyon, 7, 17, 81, 82
Grand Teton, 88, 103
Greenacres, 34, 38
Griffon College, 47
grizzly bear, 13, 44, 119, 120, 163, 206

H

Haida Indians, 45
Harrison, 7, 17, 61-65, 87, 205, 213
Harrison Centennial Celebration, 61
Harrison Marina, 61
Hatheume Lake, 96, 115

Hawaii, 83, 207
Headless Valley, 145, 150
Hecetta Lighthouse Station, 71
Henley Aerodrome, 33
Hood River, 72
Horse Ranch Range, 16
Howard's Pass, 143
Hudson Bay Glacier, 28, 197, 200
Hudson Bay Store, 18-21, 125, 158, 196
Hudson Hope, 13, 120
Hurricane Ridge, 59
Hyland Post, 24

I

Idaho, 33-35, 38, 44, 61, 81, 87, 88, 93, 102,
    103, 117, 201, 205-207, 209
Inchelium, 96, 108
Inuit, 9, 15, 29, 94
Issaquah, 32, 33, 57
Ivar's Fish Bar, 41

J

Jackson Hole, 88, 103
John Muir Trail, 68
Jonathan Livingston Seagull, 46

K

Kalispel Indian Reservation, 102
Kamloops, 99, 101, 111, 202
Kechika, 13, 119, 163, 165, 166
Kelowna, 100, 111, 202
Kenmore Air Harbor, 42, 59
Kenmore Aviation, 57
Kenny Dam, 28, 118
Kinaskan Lake, 23
King County, 33
Kingston, 41, 49
Kingston Ferry, 49
KIRO Radio, 48, 57, 58
Kispiox Valley, 25, 44
Klamath Falls, 73, 74
Klickitat County, 79
Klondike, 15, 136, 138, 139, 141, 181-184

Klondike Gold Rush, 136, 184
Klondike River, 136, 138, 139, 182
Kluane National Park, 176, 177, 181
KXLY radio, 36

L

Lake Coeur d'Alene, 7, 61-65, 87, 88, 90, 205
Lake Crescent, 51
Lake Havasu, 44, 56, 67, 87
Lake Pend Oreille, 103-105
Lake Quinault Lodge, 26, 53, 54, 56
Lake Roosevelt, 95, 102, 108
Lake Sammamish High School, 33
Lake Union, 35, 40, 41
Las Vegas, 68
Laslui Lake, 194
Liard River, 13, 16, 119-121, 133, 143, 155,
    157, 163
Liberty Lake, 34, 37, 64, 81, 90
Likely Café, 73
London Bridge, 44
loon, 13, 95-97, 107, 119, 127, 143, 209, 212
Loon and Deer lakes, 107
Luscombe, 79, 80

M

Mackenzie Mountains, 16, 147, 152, 158
Mackenzie River, 13-15, 119, 120, 136, 196
Malena Mojica, 35
Mamer and Schreck Flying Service, 203
Manitoba, 43
Maryhill Museum, 77, 78
Mayo, 134, 135, 141
McClure Lake, 27, 28, 43, 117, 119, 196,
    198-200
McDame, 16
McMillan River, 141
McQueston River, 135
Mead Airport, 95
Meek Lake, 16
Mexico, 35
Meziadin Lake, 25
Miami, 31

Mica Peak, 81
Million Dollar Valley, 162
Minto Lake, 135
Missoula, 81
Modac Indians, 74
Modoc National Wildlife Refuge, 73
Mono Lake, 67-70
Montana, 13, 44, 81, 88, 103, 120
Moodie Lake, 163-167
moose, 13, 15, 25, 26, 97, 101, 119, 147-149, 153, 154, 158, 196
Moose Ponds, 148, 149
Mount Adams, 79, 80
Mount Fujiyama, 70
Mount Hood, 78, 79
Mount Rainier, 79
Mount St. Helens, 79
Mount Thomlinson, 26
mountain goat, 13, 119
Mt. Mazama, 74
Mt. Morgan, 67
Mt. Shasta, 70
MV Tarahne, 189

N

Nahanni Butte, 145, 146, 149, 150, 153, 155
Nahanni River, 33, 39, 129, 140, 147-151, 158
Naili Cho, 148
Nass River, 25
Never Cry Wolf, 189
New England Air Museum, 65
New Zealand, 41, 53, 170
Newfoundland, 43
Newman Lake, 36, 64
Norman Wells, 14, 189
North and South Twin Lakes, 96, 108
Northern Flight of Dreams, 2, 9, 37, 47, 108, 117, 204
Northwest Christian High School, 26, 38, 60, 112
Northwest Company, 14
Northwest Territorial Outfitters, 37
Northwest Territories, 2, 8, 9, 14, 29, 33, 37, 39, 67, 94, 113, 123, 129, 131, 136, 140, 142, 147, 155, 161, 190, 228
Nova Scotia, 43

NW Territories, 1, 3

O

Okanogan Lake, 99, 111, 115
Old Crow, 9, 15, 21, 29, 94, 100, 133, 137, 139, 140
Olympic Mountains, 41, 46
Olympic National Forest, 54
Olympic Rain Forest, 7, 53, 55, 60
Omineca Air Service, 27, 28, 194, 197, 200
Ontario, 43
Ootsa Lake, 28, 118
Oregon, 43, 65-67, 70-73
Otter, 17, 158, 160, 190, 191

P

Pacific Ocean, 16, 54, 59, 199, 201
Pacific Pipeline, 45, 48, 57
Parade Magazine, 27
Parsnip River, 120
Peace River, 13, 120
Pend Oreille River, 102, 103
Penticton, 93, 95, 98, 99, 101, 108, 109, 111, 202
Penticton Airport, 99
Pima Air Museum, 83, 87
Piper Cherokees, 70
Piper J-3 Cub, 34, 104, 209
Plateau Lake, 162
Poose Capays, 97, 126
Port Angeles, 49, 50, 59
Port Townsend, 41
Portland, 43, 71, 136
Prairie Creek, 150
Priest Lake, 102, 209-212
Prince Edward Island, 43
Prince George, 115, 116
Puget Sound, 40, 41, 45-47, 89, 116

Q

Quebec, 43

R

Red Baron, 203
Red Beaver, 2, 9, 32, 33, 35-37, 39-41, 44, 48,
    49, 53, 58, 72, 73, 80, 81, 83, 88, 90, 91,
    94, 107, 124, 127-130, 134, 147, 148,
    150-152, 157, 162, 206, 208, 228
Red Lion Inn, 43
Reno, 67
Ritzville, 40
Riversong Café, 18
Rock Gardens, 149
Rocky Mountain Trench, 13, 113, 115,
    119-121, 165
Rocky Mountains, 13, 14, 64, 88, 120, 161, 167
Ross River, 133, 134
Royal Canadian Air Force, 2, 111
Royal Canadian Mounted Police, 126, 127, 163

S

S.S. Keno, 139
San Francisco, 68, 136, 181
Saskatchewan, 43
Sawmill Lake, 18, 22
Sawyer Glaciers, 24
Scatter River Airstrip, 162
Scoop Lake, 121, 163-165
Scott Field, 101, 111
Sea Bee, 64
Seattle, 18, 27, 33-35, 37, 41, 43, 45, 47, 48,
    53, 57-59, 91, 101, 112, 136, 182
Seattle Post-Intelligencer, 45, 47, 57, 58
Sergeant Preston, 135, 184, 185
Sifton Pass, 13, 119, 120
Silver Lake Mall, 35
Silverwood, 33
Simon Frazer Hotel, 28
Skagway, 8, 98, 99, 176-179, 181-187, 189
Skaha Lake, 111
Skyway Café, 36, 93
Slavey Indians, 153
sled dogs, 14
Smithers, 20, 23, 27, 28, 43, 99, 112, 130, 192,
    193, 196, 197, 199, 200
South Nahanni River, 33, 129, 140, 147, 150,
    151

Spenser Aviation, 98
spirit owl, 19, 20, 125
Spokane, 4, 9, 10, 14, 26, 29, 32-40, 56, 61, 62,
    65, 74, 79-81, 87, 89, 90, 93, 95, 101, 107,
    108, 112, 125, 126, 150, 200-203, 207,
    209, 228
Spokane Point, 61
Spokane River, 36, 95, 107
Spokane Valley, 34, 38-40, 87, 93, 101, 209
Stevens Lake, 25, 44
Stikine Plateau, 120
Stikine River, 16, 18, 19, 193, 194
Stinson 165, 64
stone sheep, 13, 119, 170
Stonehenge, 76, 77, 79
Super Cub, 64, 100, 112, 130, 196, 199
Sweden, 34

T

Tacoma, 57, 207
Tahltan Indian Village, 18
Tahltan Outfitters, 17
Takla Post, 198
Tanzilla River, 17
Tatlatuie Lake, 120
Taylor Crafts, 64
Telegraph Creek, 17-20, 22-24, 125, 126
Terrace, 27
The Dalles, 71, 72
Thompson River, 101
Thutade Lake, 120, 196
Tioga Pass, 70
Tombstone Cemetery, 83
Toronto, 31
Tubbs Hill, 90
Tuktoyaktuk, 9, 15, 21, 29, 94
Turkey, 63
Tyee Lake, 28, 200

U

United States, 2, 4, 9, 25, 63, 75, 91, 98, 101,
    111, 112, 123, 141
University of Montana, 81

Upper Klamath Lake, 74
USS Hassayampa, 41, 45, 49, 83
Utah, 44, 81

V

Vancouver, 42, 43, 50, 54, 165, 189
Victoria, 18, 21, 49, 50
Victoria Lake, 18, 21
Virginia Falls, 133, 140, 145-149, 158

W

Waldenbooks, 48
Washington state, 34, 40, 54, 89, 103, 118, 202
Washington State University, 34
Watson Lake, 2, 14, 16, 17, 21, 31, 32, 36, 37,
     53, 96, 97, 113, 114, 116, 117, 119,
     121-130, 134, 140-146, 149, 150, 157, 160,
     161, 165, 167, 174, 184, 185, 188, 189,
     208
Watson Lake Flying Service, 2, 17, 31, 32, 36,
     125, 127-129, 134, 142, 144, 165, 167, 208

Watson Lake Hotel, 97, 125, 126
Whitehorse, 15, 36, 123, 124, 133, 134, 165,
     170, 173, 181, 189, 190, 192
William C. Steele Center, 74
Williams Lake, 28, 99, 109, 111, 115, 116, 130,
     200-202
Williams Lake Airport, 28, 201, 202
Williston Lake, 13, 116-120
wolf, 13, 119, 189, 196, 197
Wrangell, 16
Wyoming, 88, 103

Y

Yellowstone, 88
Yosemite Park, 70
Yukon, 1-3, 7-9, 13-17, 29, 31, 36, 43, 58, 59,
     83, 94, 96, 100, 103, 105, 107, 110, 115,
     119, 120, 123-129, 133, 136-141, 145, 155,
     157, 163, 173, 176-178, 181-184, 188, 189,
     201, 228
Yukon Territory, 14, 16, 31, 43, 100, 123, 173,
     177, 182, 189

About the Author

Larry Whitesitt has had a passion for airplanes and flying since he was a boy. He was born in 1938 in Spokane, Washington.

In the late 1950s, he served onboard the U.S. Navy oil tanker U.S.S. Hassayampa AO-145 and was honorably discharged. In 1959, he married, had a son, and learned to fly. He moved to Canada in 1964 with his family. His dream was to build a cabin and live off the land in the wilderness.

During the 1960s and 1970s, he was a bush pilot in British Columbia, the Yukon, and Northwest Territories in Canada. His first book, *Flight of the Red Beaver,* was published in 1990. The book recounts his adventures flying de Havilland Beaver float planes and ski planes.

He now lives in Fairfield, Washington, near Spokane. He is semi-retired and enjoys hiking, kayaking, and flying with his three grandchildren. He is currently writing a novel about a bush pilot in the Yukon in the 1940s and 1950s.